P9-CPZ-521

THE CHURCH & WORLD MISSION

MAX WARD RANDALL,
115 INSTITUTE DR.,
LINCOLN, IL. 62656

By the same author

Consistent Christianity
Take my life
Give up your small ambitions
Cinderella with amnesia

MICHAEL GRIFFITHS

ZONDERVAN
PUBLISHING HOUSE OF THE ZONDERVAN CORPORATION
GRAND RAPIDS, MICHIGAN 49506

Library of Congress Cataloging in Publication Data

Griffiths, Michael, 1928-
    The church and world mission.

    Originally published: Shaking the sleeping beauty. 1980.
    Includes bibliographical references.
    1. Missions—Addresses, essays, lectures.   2. Church growth
— Addresses, essays, lectures.   3. Christianity and culture — Ad-
dresses, essays, lectures.   4. Church and the world — Addresses,
essays, lectures.   I. Title.
BV2070.G74   1982   266   82-10981
ISBN 0-310-45111-6

Awake, awake,
Clothe yourself in your strength, O Zion;
Clothe yourself in your beautiful garments
Is. 52:1

And this do, knowing the time, that it is already the
hour for you to awaken from sleep
Rom. 13:11

The people of the future
Tertullian

The Church is like an arrow sent out into the world to
point to the future
Moltmann

Contents

Chief abbreviations

AV	Authorized (King James) Version of the Bible
CIM	China Inland Mission, now the Overseas Missionary Fellowship
EMQ	*Evangelical Missions Quarterly*
ET	English translation
LTEHHV	*Let the Earth Hear His Voice*. Official report of the 1974 Lausanne International Congress on World Evangelization.
LXX	The Septuagint (pre-Christian Greek version of the Old Testament)
OMF	Overseas Missionary Fellowship
RSV	Revised Standard Version of the Bible
SPG	Society for the Propagation of the Gospel
WCC	World Council of Churches
IRM	*International Review of Mission*. Journal of the Commission on World Mission and Evangelism of the World Council of Churches

Author's preface

This book contains the substance of the 1978 Chavasse Lectures given at Wycliffe Hall, Oxford, in January, February and March of that year. I am grateful to the Principal, the Rev. Jim Hickinbotham, for his encouragement in seeking a publisher and to all the members of Wycliffe Hall for being such patient listeners, and especially for their further comments and questions which have stimulated my own thought.

The material in these lectures has been hammered into shape through the courtesy of other groups of Christians particularly at the Fiftieth Jubilee of the Baptist College of New Zealand in 1976 and the Sixtieth Anniversary of the College of Bible and Missions in Croydon, New South Wales, in the same year. Most of the ideas have been refined with the successive orientation courses for newly arrived missionaries of the Overseas Missionary Fellowship held in Singapore three times each year. Each new occasion prompts new ideas and development so that I owe a good deal to my fellow missionaries, as well as to a host of writers and speakers, only some of whom are directly quoted in the text.

In reworking the material we have also deliberately provided suggestions for further reading and possible questions for seminar discussions at the end of each chapter, hoping to improve the suitability of the book for missions courses in theological and Bible colleges. I hope this will whet students' appetites to read more books about mission.

Chapter 5, 'The grace of God for planting and perfecting churches', contains material found in greater detail in *Cinderella's Betrothal Gifts* (OMF, 1978), but written as it were from the opposite end, considering what abilities are required for planting and perfecting churches, and seeing that the New Testament stresses 'grace and power' rather than human methodology.

It is worth adding the caveat that quotation of an author does not mean endorsement or agreement with all or even many of his writings. This is especially true of chapter 4 where the writers profusely quoted illustrate positions which I believe to be seriously in error.

My especial thanks are due to Mary Wilcox who typed and retyped this manuscript not only long after office hours but even after she had ceased to work for the OMF at all.

Guildford, June 1979

Introduction

The study of missions is really the study of the church on a world-wide canvas, and as such it gives purpose and meaning to theological study. A room full of theological students always reminds me of a swarm of caterpillars assiduously chewing up leaves on the trees. Can they, I wonder, realize what all this eating is in aid of? The consumption of theological leaves is so absorbing a task in itself that these theological caterpillars preparing for the ministry can lose sight of the trees, let alone the great forest over which they are to fly as butterflies in the days ahead. This book will give you the opportunity to raise your heads for a moment from the all-absorbing consumption of leaves in the theological library, to remind you of the goal and purpose for which you are training. If you cannot see what the church is for or where she is going, then all your study loses its point. *The study of missions brings everything into focus. You lose the sense of merely timelessly continuing the liturgical worship of the church: you move into a world where there is a sense of urgency, of limited time in which to work and to achieve your goals. There is a task to be finished without delay.* It demands the immediate application in concrete terms of all the things we so easily study in theory.

The study of missions – the relatively new discipline sometimes being called 'missiology' – is much more than a mere branch of recent church history. It is the most

exciting cross-disciplinary subject *par excellence,* cross-fer-
tilizing most other branches of theology. It requires a
careful study of biblical text (see Appendix), hermeneutics
(chapter 4) and theology (chapter 5). The missionary
requires an understanding of the philosophy of religion
and Christian apologetics for fruitful confrontation with
other religious systems. The principles of Christian education are crucial for the training of church leadership.
We discover the most fascinating relationship between
missions and eschatology (chapter 6) as we try to define
the goals of completed mission and perfected church.
What are the intermediate stages to be anticipated
between the churches as they are today and the perfected
Christian community when it welcomes its returning King
for his royal visit? How will the church develop as the
parousia approaches? The study of missions also brings
church history up to date, and demands a knowledge of
young churches whose history has not been written up in
any detail. Understanding the cultural environment of the
church is also crucial, and thus has arisen the 'contextualization' debate (chapter 2), although I prefer to call
it 'de-indigenization'.

Any church which relegates mission to being the peripheral activity of a lunatic fringe of enthusiasts is doomed
to self-destruction. Emil Brunner had it right when he
said that 'the Church exists by mission as a fire exists by
burning', and it was this concept that gave the title to the
series of Chavasse Lectures, 'The Church Incandescent'.
The church which has lost its concern for mission is down
to its ember days amidst the institutional ashes. It needs
the fresh breath of the Spirit of God to fan its dying
embers back into life.

At times I have felt free to disagree strongly with current views which seem to me to be dangerously lop-sided
biblically. Current ecumenical theology stresses creation,
incarnation and resurrection but tends to ignore the fall,
atonement and judgment. Heterodoxy need not involve
the teaching of positive error, but the wilful and deliberate

12

omission of half of historic Christian truth. Some Christian thinking on mission seems to have lost its way and the passion for the evangelization of the world and the salvation of the lost seems to have diminished – thus the section on the 'Trojan Horse' of universalism (chapter 4).

An earlier generation of missionaries never expected to return home, but was determined to do its utmost to preach Christ before being carried off by diseases for which there was little in the way either of prophylaxis or cure. They were not much interested in the euthanasia of mission, moratoria or short-term service. They were mainly short-termers because they had no choice and died in the full flush of youth, while still seeking to understand language and culture. It seems tragic that now at last when most of these practical problems have been overcome, the enemy strategy of undermining the whole motivation of the missionary movement is little recognized. Jonah still doesn't want to go to Nineveh, but instead of going down to Joppa and making off in the opposite direction he stays at home and tells us that the day of missions is past.

Probably in recent years the most significant, if uncomfortable and disturbing, voice on missions has come from Dr Donald McGavran, the founder and now the Dean Emeritus of the School of Church Growth and World Mission at Fuller Seminary in Pasadena, California. McGavran first addressed himself to the older denominational churches with their swarm of satellite organizations, hopelessly bogged down in a morass of institutions, committees and theological uncertainties, who seemed to have lost their way and forgotten the object of their journey.

The following sample from his writing shows why a whole later issue of the *International Review of Mission* (*IRM*, the ecumenical organ of the Commission on World Mission and Evangelism of the World Council of Churches) was devoted to trying to shoot him down.

The crisis in missions is this: it is possible to wax enthusiastic about factory evangelism, confrontation, dialogue, the whole gospel, the whole man and many other good things, without intending or achieving any planting of new churches, or winning any unbelievers to the Christian faith. Mission . . . becomes witness, outreach, rapprochement, penetration – there is no limit to the vague, elastic words which have only one thing in common: they do not require the baptism of bodies, the salvation of souls and the building of visible new churches.[1]

. . . This strategy is really a defence of the existing machine of mission, its departments, vested interests, bureaucracies and massive service arms. These all shelter under slogans such as 'the whole gospel', 'all its fullness' and 'the whole man'. No one doubts that there is a whole gospel, but that is not the issue. The issue is whether the apostles shall wait on tables. The issue is whether Paul at Troas, hearing 'Come over to Macedonia and help us', shall send over some specialists to enter into dialogue with the priests of Jove and Venus, and others to assist a revolt against Roman oppression and slave holding. The issue is that, while we proclaim 'the whole gospel' to 'the whole man', opportunities for propagating the Christian religion are neglected. Opportunity after opportunity to win the winnable while they are winnable and to multiply churches in receptive populations is lost. Certainly, the whole gospel is good. Balanced rations for sheep are good – but the only sheep who can be fed with such rations are those that have first been found and brought into the fold. The whole gospel for all mankind means little, unless it is preceded by stupendous church planting. The gospel is empty words until it is believed and obeyed. Christ died for all, but vast multitudes do not know this; and many who do know, reject him. Only those who are baptized into Christ and become responsible members of his body are made into new creatures. This strategy of the fifties is theologically and bib-

[1] D. A. McGavran, 'Wrong Strategy: The Real Crisis in Missions', *IRM*, October 1965, p.456.

lically wrong. It does not throb with Christ's passion for men's eternal redemption. It makes haste to point out that there are many kinds of redemption and appears equally in favour of all. It does not blaze with certainty that man, the immortal soul, was created in the image of God, is not in that image now and must regain it through the saving work of Christ. It does not seem to know which part of Christian religion is centre and which is periphery. It loses the purpose for which the organization was created in maintaining the organization to carry out the purpose.[2]

You can see why McGavran and his school are not popular in the circles he so rightly criticizes. But the questions he raises are real questions. Do we *now* know better than the apostles what Christianity is all about? What are the goals and objectives of mission in the Bible? There are biblical reasons why the church should grow, related to the purposes of God. The danger of a simplistic view of church growth is that it concentrates upon measurable goals – numbers of baptisms or of newly planted churches – without asking the important questions about the quality of the converts and still more about the qualitative growth of the congregations into which those converts are introduced. Thus the critics of McGavran make some real points in reply; but it is not a question of having quantitative measurable growth and qualitative growth as alternatives – both forms of growth are equally biblical and equally essential.

In an earlier book on the subject of the church[3] I suggested that the problem of the church is that it sits like Cinderella amid the institutional ashes suffering from a severe lapse of memory. It has forgotten where it is meant to be going. In this book (more or less charitably, I am not sure) I am suggesting that the church is asleep, surrounded by dense hedges of cultural tradition. Cinderella

[2] *Ibid.* p.454.
[3] M. C. Griffiths, *Cinderella with Amnesia* (IVP, 1975).

seems to have forgotten about the Prince. Sleeping Beauty seems to be unaware that the 'Prince of Life' (Acts 3:15) stands at the door and knocks, urging the church to repent and admit its poverty and need (Rev. 3:15–20). The Bible does not see the bride of Christ as merely waiting passively in the knowledge that 'some day my prince will come,' whereupon she will rise immediately as beautiful as the day she fell asleep under the curse. She is to perfect holiness in the fear of God, to seek to be without spot and blameless, and having this hope to purify herself even as he is pure. The New Testament is full of calls to wake up and stay alert for the coming of the bridegroom. So the purpose of this book is to seek to rouse and shake ecclesiastical Sleeping Beauty to a fresh sense of her mission in the world.

1 Church and growth

I planted, Apollos watered, but God was causing the growth. So then neither the one who plants nor the one who waters is anything, but God who causes the growth. Now he who plants and he who waters are one; but each will receive his own reward according to his own labour. For we are God's fellow-workers; you are God's field, God's building.

According to the grace of God which was given to me, as a wise master builder I laid a foundation, and another is building upon it. But let each man be careful how he builds upon it. For no man can lay a foundation other than the one which is laid, which is Jesus Christ. Now if any man builds upon the foundation with gold, silver, precious stones, wood, hay, straw, each man's work will become evident; for the day will show it, because it is to be revealed with fire; and the fire itself will test the quality of each man's work. If any man's work which he has built upon it remains, he shall receive a reward. If any man's work is burned up, he shall suffer loss; but he himself shall be saved, yet so as through fire.

Do you not know that you are a temple of God, and that the Spirit of God dwells in you? If any man destroys the temple of God, God will destroy him, for the temple of God is holy, and that is what you are. 1 Cor. 3:6–17

Even a sleeping beauty grows while she sleeps, but what quality of growth will that be? Physical only? Social? Spiritual?

God causes the church, his bride, to grow.

Paul's description in I Corinthians 3 of the ministry in which he and the other apostles were engaged makes it clear that God gives the growth (verses 6–7). The word *theos* is in the emphatic position: '*God's* fellow workers we are; *God's* agricultural project (*georgion*) you are; *God's* building project you are' (verse 9). It is 'according to the *grace of God*' that Paul has laid the foundation of the local church in Corinth (verse 10). It is *God's* temple which is being established (verse 16).

Some writers oppose the activism of Donald McGavran and the church growth school, which they see as part of the American obsession with success and growth applying its pragmatism and methodology even to spiritual affairs. They stress over against this, the *missio Dei*, that God himself is the missionary God sending his Son as a missionary Christ. This emphasis is clearly good and right.

> To speak of God's action in the world is, however, to refer to mission, for mission is not something which the church 'does'; it is a divine movement in which the church has to be involved if it is true to its calling. The church's role is not to concern itself about its own growth, but to facilitate, to identify and to participate in this movement . . . the church's vocation is to join in God's action in the world as he continues his movement of humanization, assisting man towards that maturity or fullness embodied in Christ.[1]

But is he right that the church is not to be concerned about its own growth or lack of it?

The biblical passage above suggests several answers. The first answer is that the *church must grow*, precisely because it is God's will and purpose *to cause it to grow*. He has promised that he will build his church. The gates of hell will not prevail against it, though they may certainly try. There is to be a great multitude, which no man can number, of every tribe, tongue and nation before the

[1] J. G. Davies, 'Church Growth: a Critique', *IRM*, July 1968, pp.297, 294.

throne and before the Lamb (Rev. 7:9). It was precisely because 'the hand of the Lord was with them' in Antioch that 'a large number who believed turned to the Lord' (Acts 11:21). This is surely self-evident.

We have already mentioned the edition of *IRM* (July 1968) primarily devoted to shooting down McGavran's church growth ideas, and J. G. Davies in his helpful critique raises several objections:

1. To define the goal of mission as church growth is an ecclesiastical narrowing of the concept of the kingdom of God. 'The church is an instrument of the kingdom, or should be; it may also be conceived as the first fruits of the kingdom, but it is not to be identified with the kingdom, which is what we are doing if we rest with church growth as our objective.'

2. Planning for church growth is limiting the free activity of the Holy Spirit. We are putting a human plan in the place of the *missio Dei*. We demonstrate a lack of faith by trusting in human activity to promote church growth.

3. 'To think in terms of church growth is to plan for survival and this is the antithesis of the pattern of life laid down for us by Christ. That life was one of service and suffering unto death, of self-giving and not self-aggrandisement, of acceptance of the cross and not self-sufficiency.'

This last point seems a little unfair. It is a peculiar reversal to produce the paradoxical concept of 'church death' as an example of selfless sacrifice, so that self-immolation is presented as God's purpose for the church (which is not exactly the force of 1 Cor. 3:17, which promises destruction to anybody destroying a local temple of God's people – 'and that is what you [the congregation in Corinth] are'). Taking biblical ideas out of context creates a nonsense.

What about the objection that it confuses the church and the kingdom? In passages like Colossians 1:12–14, Paul does appear to identify the forgiven saints with the presently existing kingdom of Christ. We grant that the church is not to be identified with the kingdom. But we insist that both alike are part of the sure sovereign purpose of God, being brought about by the *missio Dei*. We may grant that the final and real goal of the *missio Dei* is the establishment of God's kingdom. But we observe that the church is the way and the means by which he accomplishes his sovereign purpose.

Even an elementary familiarity with the New Testament shows the apostles after Pentecost, as well as Paul and his associates, travelling tirelessly and labouring ceaselessly to plant new churches and perfect them. They do not seem to hold views of the kingdom which cause them to lose interest in church growth. On the contrary, their lives are risked and their energies expended for the task of planting and building the churches. Philip preached the good news about the kingdom of God and large numbers of Samaritan men and women were baptized (Acts 8:12). After encouraging disciples to continue in the faith saying that 'through many tribulations we must enter the kingdom of God' they appointed elders for them in every church (Acts 14:22). Indeed 'preaching the kingdom' (Acts 20:25; 28:23, 31) seems to be a straightforward synonym for evangelism and church planting. The very biblical usage of 'preaching the kingdom' is tied in with church growth. Belonging to the kingdom is the consequence of evangelism (Col. 1:13), so that Davies' first objection does not seem fair.

At first sight, the suggestion that human planning for church growth is a limitation of the free activity of the Holy Spirit seems a spiritual one to which we must be sympathetic. Davies is echoing the same anxiety which we share with Padilla (see p. 145) about the obsession with efficiency and computer technology shown by some American missiologists. We recognize that quoting statistical data proves very little and achieves absolutely nothing. But here in this very passage, which stresses so strongly divine sovereignty in giving church growth, there is the clear implication that man has a responsibility before God for the state of the churches, and cannot escape into quietism by giving submission to divine sovereignty as the reason for shoddy church building or doing nothing at all. We cannot blame God for wood, hay and stubble, still less for demolition. We are to be judged in that day by the quality of our work directed towards church growth and church building, and to this we now turn. For the same passage in Corinthians that teaches us God's sovereignty in church growth also stresses *man's responsibility for the state of the church* and progress of the gospel. It seems difficult to escape the force of the passage.

Paul and Apollos are servants to whom the Lord gives opportunity (verse 5) and that means that Paul plants and then Apollos waters (verse 6); that Paul lays a foundation and then a nameless 'another' (probably Cephas) builds upon it (verse 10). The apostle-missionary is to be a 'wise master-builder' and there follows the serious warning: 'But let each man be careful *how* he builds upon it.' The passage then goes on to explain the frightening latitude which God in his sovereignty has allowed to man to mess up God's own church. He may be wise and build with gold, silver and precious building stone (verse 12); or foolish, like the first two of Disney's little pigs who built with wood, hay and straw (verse 12b). The solemn reminder that 'the day' will test the *quality* of each man's work (verse 13; we shall come back to this matter of quality) is followed by the even more solemn reminder that the local church is a temple of God, indwelt by the Spirit of God, but that 'if any man destroys the temple of God, God will destroy him' (verse 17). You cannot refuse human responsibility for building the church which God has entrusted to man, even though it is his building project. He gives both opportunity and grace to the wise master-builder who asks for them.

It seems then that we Christians must accept responsibility for the state of the churches and the progress of mission, and that we cannot, biblically, blame God for either. We must not allow an overstress on the antitheses between church and kingdom, divine sovereignty and human responsibility or the *missio Dei* and the *missio ecclesiae* to excuse our burying our heads in the sand. The kingdom is the reign of God and he is sovereign. But the church is the gathering (*Sammlung*) and sending (*Sendung*) of men and we are responsible for it before God, because he himself chooses to make us so.

Quantitative dimensions of growth
In what ways can the church be said to grow?

1. NUMERICAL GROWTH (Acts 2:41; 5:14; 6:7)

. . . and there were added that day about three thousand souls. . . . multitudes of men and women were constantly added to their number; . . . and the number of disciples continued to increase greatly.

You cannot build the new temple without bricks or living stones. You cannot build up a body without members. Evangelism, then, must be a part of mission and the prerequisite for the other parts of mission. Some are still defensively hostile to the concept of individual conversion, which seems like an evangelical ploy to imply that liberals have no personal experience. It is clear, however, that Acts relates to us the account of five individual conversions in some detail.[2]

While households joined with Cornelius, Lydia and the jailer, there are no such indications for the Ethiopian eunuch, or for Saul, of whose individual conversion the Spirit provides no less than three accounts in Acts. John Stott devoted one of his 1975 Chavasse Lectures to this subject of conversion and another to evangelism, which should be consulted if we have any difficulties on this point.[3]

[2] See Stephen Smalley's excellent article, 'Conversion in the New Testament', *Churchman*, September 1964, p.200.

[3] John Stott, *Christian Mission in the Modern World* (Falcon, 1975).

The missionary has always needed to be an evangelist before he could become a teacher. The cultural problems associated with this will be considered in the next chapter.

2. MULTIPLYING OF CONGREGATIONS (Acts 9:31; 16:5)

So the church throughout all Judea and Galilee and Samaria enjoyed peace, being built up. . . So the churches were being strengthened in the faith, and were increasing in number daily.

It is not enough to save souls and baptize bodies; they must be built into new visible congregations.

There remains a great deal of church planting to be done, often alongside existing churches. At the Lausanne International Congress on World Evangelization, Ralph Winter pointed out that 95% of the members of the Church of South India come from only five out of more than a hundred social classes.[4] The fact that some kind of national church exists is not enough. That is only a foothold or, as someone has described it, 'a beach-head'. This latter concept is well illustrated by my own experience as a theological student when we used to pray for a bishop in Iran who was a former member of the college. I had assumed that if there was an established national church with a national bishop, then the church must be well developed. However, recent reference to the *World Christian Handbook* revealed that this particular bishop was only responsible for a church of 400 communicant members and indeed that the total membership of all Christian churches in Iran is no more than 5,000 in a country with a population of 35 millions. A tiny beach-head indeed where only one person in 7,000 is a professing believer. Recent events have shown how vulnerable this church is. In many countries of the world the churches are confined within certain ethnic groups (as in Malaysia, Indonesia or Cyprus) or within certain geographical areas (in cities

---

[4] Ralph D. Winter, 'The Highest Priority: Cross-Cultural Evangelism' in *Let the Earth Hear His Voice* (hereafter *LTEHHV*, World Wide Publications, Minneapolis, 1975), p.214.

in Japan) or social classes (India, as mentioned above, or Laos). A huge task of church planting still has to be achieved.

Usually when people speak of church growth it is this quantitative and measurable church growth which they have in mind. We can find statistics of the numbers of 'decisions', baptisms or congregations. But this gives rise to legitimate criticism about the *quality* of such growth and we have already seen that this is a proper biblical concern. If a church of a hundred half-hearted members grows into a church of two hundred half-hearted members, how much has it grown? Thus, criticizing McGavran, Davies points out that the church in Britain maintains a dichotomy between its religion and everyday life and asks 'Is this the church whose growth we are to promote?'[5]

Above all facts and figures, the *authenticity* of conversion to Christ is of supreme importance. Indeed, a too rapid numerical growth can create serious problems both in this important matter of authenticity and with regard to the future development of the church in any given situation.

In Indonesia the Pantya Cila (Five Points of the Constitution) gives first place to 'reverence for Godhead' so that monotheism, and thus Islam and Christianity, is the national prestige belief. There is, not surprisingly, a not inconsiderable movement from animism to monotheism. But which religion is to be preferred? If the animist is fond of eating pork (and many villages have more pigs than people) then he prefers to become a Christian, however inadequate the motives. There need not be any work of the Spirit in regeneration to produce this quality of 'convert'. It was of this kind of problem that A. J. Gordon wrote: 'If perchance the church should attract men, without at the same time transforming them; if she shall attach them to her membership without assimilating them to her life, she has only weakened herself by her increase and

[5] Davies, *IRM*, July 1968, p.292.

diminished herself by her addition.' The real problem is that such *qualitative* growth is much harder to assess and not readily capable of *quantitative* measurement.[6] But this is the 'quality of each man's work' which God is going to test in the lives of those called to the ministry. (A word study of apostolic activity, in the appendix to this book, answers the question, 'What did the apostles do and to what did they give their energies?')

Qualitative dimensions of growth

It is not enough to increase the number of bricks or even of piles of bricks. Those bricks must be laid together on the foundation and erected into a building. In the same way, a body is not just a heap of meat, but a living being in which all the members work effectively together. Thus we are not concerned merely with the dimensions of body mass, but with considerations of quality and health, so that physique, muscle tone and co-ordination become critical. Sadly, this seems to be a dimension which has been neglected by ecumenicals and evangelicals alike. Ecumenicals have reacted against evangelical criticism of institutionalism and nominal Christians, while evangelicals have tended to put so much stress upon evangelism and conversions that they have been, until recently, less concerned about the quality of congregational life and worship.

3. GROWTH IN LOVE AND INTERPERSONAL
RELATIONSHIPS (Eph. 4:16; Phil. 1:9; 1 Thes. 3:12)

The whole body . . . upbuilds itself in love (RSV). *I pray that your* (plural) *love may abound still more and more in real knowledge and all discernment; . . . and may the Lord cause you to increase and abound in love for one another, and for all men.*
These verses provide evidence of a significant recurrent

[6] *Pace* Ralph Winter who argues from ice cream that quantity must always have some quality while quality can attach itself only to a measurable quantity: 'Quality or Quantity' in D. McGavran (ed.) *Crucial Issues in Missions Tomorrow* (Moody Press, 1972).

theme in the New Testament churches. Paul reminds the Corinthians that while the gifts of the Spirit will pass away the fruit of the Spirit, which is love, will not. Rather than the 'drive-in' church where people need not even meet each other, Christians are expected to relate to each other. Congregations may progress from the artificiality of formal greetings to the reality of genuine interpersonal relationships in the household of God, where friends know that love of brothers (*philadelphia*) and can express it in practical ways in everyday congregational life.

4. GROWTH IN CONGREGATIONAL CO-OPERATION AS A BODY (Eph. 4:12–13, 16)

. . . for the equipping of the saints for the work of service, to the building up of the body of Christ; until we all attain to the unity of the faith . . . according to the proper working of each individual part, [which] causes the growth of the body for the building up of itself in love.

A body in which only one member is functioning is nearly dead and taken off to hospital. The one-man-band concept of the church is a cultural hangover from the days in Britain and elsewhere when the squire and the parson were the only literate people in the parish capable of reading the prayers and the Bible lessons. Roy Castle is credited in the *Guinness Book of Records* with playing forty different musical instruments in four minutes: what an illustration of the omnicompetent one-man-band minister!

How few congregations there are where a lot of members are exercising functions. Often the majority of members are passive spectators and auditors of the religious professional's performance. There is a 'mutual collusion in dependence' between them, for some parishioners like it so, and so does the one-man-band individualist. Theological education will take a great step forward when, instead of training soloists primarily for pulpit ministry, six feet above contradiction and with a captive audience, it starts to train 'conductors' to develop the spiritual gifts of others. I belong to a church where more than three hundred Christians have roles to perform. The 'team ministry' of two or three specialists is only a beginning. Sometimes in American churches one feels that the larger staff team of specialists does more to impede the involvement of others than does even the one-man band. We must pray to develop a 'shared ministry' in which every member of the congregation can play some part. This does not imply that the functions and spiritual gifts of being a teacher or steersman cease to be important. The heart must pump blood to the other members so that they will be vitally motivated. Our *cultural view of the ministry* (for it is no more than that) may be too man-glorifying, ministering to clerical pride more than to the building up of the congregation. So mobilization and involvement of the whole congregation is another dimension in which a church may grow.

5. GROWTH IN TRAINING OF TEACHERS AND SENDING
   OUT OF MISSIONARIES (Acts 11:23, 26; 13:1; 15:35;
   Heb. 5:12)

By this time you ought to be teachers.
It is difficult to show from the Bible that there would normally be only a solitary teacher in each congregation. One classical instance is Antioch. Barnabas is sent to Antioch: so the first teacher has arrived. He promptly goes off to fetch Saul and the two of them teach the church for a year. By that time there are five! Two are then sent off as missionaries; but significantly 'Paul and Barnabas stayed in Antioch, teaching and preaching, *with many others also*, the word of the Lord.' Yet in our system one man may do all the preaching for years without ever effectively training or involving others.

A missionary in South Thailand recently worked for four years in a group of five Thai rice-growing villages. He started with four and finished with thirty-four baptized believers. What is more significant is that during that period he trained five men to accept pastoral oversight of the five villages, and to preach once a month to the whole group and once a week in one of the five villages, while continuing their normal work. One of the men left school early at sixteen. The other four left at twelve or earlier! In western countries many a minister has a congregation full of graduates, yet when he leaves after seven or ten years he has to be replaced by another minister from outside.

It is an interesting exercise to produce a list showing that nearly every New Testament congregation sent out missionaries. Antioch sent out Paul and Barnabas, Jerusalem produced Mark and Silas. From the Macedonian churches, Philippi produced Epaphroditus ('your apostle', Phil. 2:25), and probably Luke and perhaps Titus; Thessalonica sent Aristarchus and Secundus (Acts 20:4) and Berea sent Sopater. Of the churches of Asia Minor, Lystra is known to have sent out Timothy, Derbe sent Gaius and so on.

This multiplication of the number of teachers and missionaries is a significant factor in enabling the earlier goal of the mulitiplication of congregations to be achieved. One seriously questions whether the continuing stress upon the predominantly academic qualifications which require that men give up their normal professions in order to enter a full-time training institution is really in the interests of the church or even of the men who are trained there. Encouraging development of Theological Education by Extension (TEE) is a realistic missionary endeavour to grapple with this problem which ought to be considered much more seriously in countries which have long-established systems of residential training. One is not proposing the immediate dissolution of our theological monasteries, only a modest reconsideration in the interests of effective training!

6. GROWTH IN CONGREGATIONAL PROFILE WITH THE DEVELOPMENT OF CHRISTIAN FAMILIES
(Eph. 5:21, 22; 6:4)

. . . wives . . . husbands . . . children . . .
In young Asia we can have whole congregations made up of unmarried young people, mainly teenagers. The congregation is essentially a peer group. In Singapore, where the parental generation may speak a dialect and their converted children have been educated in English, there are 'churches' of two or three hundred young people with only one or two married couples. I know of similar situations both in Japan and the Philippines where the original congregation was made up almost entirely of university and high school students. Such congregations can clearly progress towards a profile which is a more representative cross-section of the population as a whole. Young people marry and start Christian homes: in this way a whole congregation is able to mature. It is here in the homes that the life of the Christian community continues during the week apart from the plenary sessions on the Sunday. The development from individuals to households and then even to extended Christian families is clearly a form of church growth which brings the congregation to a greater stability. There is an interesting congregation of seventy to eighty in Metropolitan Manila where nearly every member is a blood relation within one large extended family.

7. GROWTH IN HOLINESS AND BEAUTY OF LIFESTYLE
(2 Cor. 3:18; Eph. 5:27; 1 Thes. 3:13; 1 Thes. 5:23)

But we all, beholding as in a mirror the glory of the Lord, are being transformed into the same image from glory to glory; a beautiful church without spot or wrinkle; that He may establish your hearts unblamable in holiness; May the God of peace Himself sanctify you entirely . . . without blame at the coming of our Lord Jesus Christ.
Sanctification in biblical terms is corporate, not just indi-

vidual. The fruit of the Spirit is corporate also: *love* demands an object, *joy* an opportunity for shared verbalization, *peace* reigns over a human group, while *long-suffering* demands other Christians patiently to suffer long! The concept of a solitary saint is unknown in the New Testament: the word comes sixty-one times in the plural but only once in the singular.

The goal of congregational life in every church in any part of the world is a glorious perfected community. Congregations can grow cold and backslide just as individuals can and do. There are congregations in the Third World which are now made up of second and third generation Christians. There are areas where there have been mass turnings to the Lord but there has never been a clear rejection of animistic customs and fetishes, and where morality has never yet been recalibrated to biblical standards; where whole congregations need to progress towards holiness. Congregations can be blessed and make progress (Phil. 1:25) just as individuals can. It is something that every theological student dreams may happen in the churches in which he will one day minister. We shall be thinking more about this goal of the church when we consider eschatology and mission in the final chapter. These are surely ways in which we, if we are to become wise master-builders, will be able to build with gold, silver or precious building stone.

8. GROWTH IN CONGREGATIONAL IMPACT UPON THE SURROUNDING COMMUNITY (Phil. 1:27)

Only conduct yourselves in a manner worthy of the gospel of Christ; so that . . . I may hear of you that you are standing firm in one spirit, with one mind striving together for the faith of the gospel. While, as we shall see in a later chapter, it is a distortion to suggest that the church exists only to serve the world (the Bible makes it clear that God has a purpose for the church as such, that it is part of his plan of salvation: Mt. 1:21; Acts 15:14; 1 Pet. 2:9–10; Eph. 5:26–27; 2:22) the local church is not a ghetto: it is an *open-ended com-*

munity. Morris Stewart describes the London church for whom the major item on the agenda of their annual meeting concerned an expensive wrought iron fence and comments, 'It's not clear whether this was to keep the non-Christians out or the Christians in.' The people of God in the old covenant were intended to be a witness to the nations. The New Testament church was also concerned with those who were 'outside'.

Philippians 1:27 is an interesting verse suggesting three corporate images for the local church: living like citizens (*politeuesthe*), fighting like soldiers (*stēkete*) and striving together side by side like a team of athletes or gladiators (*sunathlountes*). Each of these corporate metaphors has much to teach us. There are civic responsibilities where Christian testimony as salt and light is crucial. There is to be impact upon society. There will be conflict too – thus the repeated use of the military metaphor with its concept of the church under attack from a hostile society. I like the athlete metaphor best: the members are united in a common aim of moving together in the face of opposition down to the opposite end of the pitch. They pass opportunities to one another, they back each other up in case any mistake is made and together they press home their attack. The point of all three metaphors, however, is surely that the church does not only grow through the long-suffering of fellow Christians in solving its own internal problems, nor even in gathering together for worship. It grows as it goes out together into the world to serve together side by side in various projects – in evangelism and outreach, in deeds of welldoing, in struggles of protest – and in doing these things together as Christians the church is made stronger. It grows by doing. Some churches have little or no local impact, others have a great deal. Here is another kind of growth then.

9. GROWTH IN DOCTRINAL UNDERSTANDING AND EXPERIENCE OF CHRISTIAN TRUTH (Col. 2:7)

Having been firmly rooted and now being built up in Him and established in your faith, just as you were instructed.

It is sadly true that there are some congregations which are theologically illiterate, without any systematic teaching ministry. They are fed, if that is the word, on haphazard, hastily prepared, devotional snacks thrown together at the last minute, more the product of professional desperation to have something to say than as a result of any clearly defined programme of teaching. Such congregations suffer from doctrinal malnutrition and dietary deficiencies. There is real progress to be made in an instructed congregation that is used to meat and not merely the elementary milk diet so often provided (1 Cor. 3:2; Heb. 5:12–14).

It should be noted, however, that in biblical thinking this 'knowledge' is not merely cerebral and cognitive, but also experimental and devotional. 'And this I pray, that your love may abound still more and more in real knowledge and sensitivity, so that you may know what is important' (Phil. 1:9–10). We need to experience what we know, and to implement what we understand.

10. GROWTH IN WORSHIP AND KNOWLEDGE OF GOD (Col. 1:9, 11–12)

. . . we have not ceased to pray for you and to ask that you may be filled with the knowledge of His will in all spiritual wisdom and understanding . . .; joyously giving thanks to the Father . . .

I have left this kind of growth to the last, not because it is least important but because it is the one that is easy to lose sight of in our enthusiasm for the growth of the church, and in our urgency for the baptism of bodies, salvation of souls and planting and perfecting of churches. The baptism is in *God*'s name, the salvation is of *God*, and the church is *his* body of which Christ is the *head*. It is all in him and through him and for him. He is its author and perfecter. The mission is his mission and the church is his church on its way to his kingdom. Thus we have to remember that *Sammlung* (gathering) and *Sendung* (sending) belong together and that each leads to the other. We all know that there are congregations where the coldness, formality and institutional deadness bring our spiritual temperatures plunging down to freezing point, while there are others where the hush of the Lord's presence is immediately sensed and our cold hearts are warmed and we are lifted up to heavenly places. We all know from experience that congregations, even though social mobility alters their constituent members, may progress in the excellence of their reality, fervour and corporate experience of God. We grow out of our customary ruts into an unforced spontaneity, warmth and reality in worshipping God together.

Conclusions

A study of the New Testament shows that while quantitative church growth is to be anticipated because God is at work to give the growth, *the biblical emphasis is at least as much upon quality as quantity*, and this is what we are encouraged to pray for. If our concern for the church is largely program-orientated, seeing the minister as a king of activities organizer at a permanent spiritual Butlins, we shall fail. Biblically-determined goal-orientation has given us a clear mandate to labour for the perfecting of the church as the great missionary task – in our own country, and in every country of the world. As new congregations are planted so these developing congregations must be perfected.

This is the chief end of mission – to plant and perfect the church. And this definition of mission, the church's prime activity of extending and upbuilding itself, is fundamental to all that follows.

Material for study

Donald G. McGavran, 'Wrong Strategy: The Real Crisis in Missions', *IRM*, October 1965.

'Church Growth', *IRM*, July 1968. Much of this issue consists of critical responses to McGavran's earlier article. Particular attention should be given to Jordan Bishop's article, 'Numerical Growth – An Adequate Criterion of Mission?', and to J. G. Davies' article, 'Church Growth: a Critique'. Considerable benefit will also be derived from reading McGavran's totally unrepentant response to these criticisms in his article 'Church Growth Strategy Continued', *IRM*, July 1968.

Ralph D. Winter, 'The Highest Priority: Cross-Cultural Evangelism', *LTEHHV*, pp.213–241.

Questions for discussion

1. Are 'the baptism of bodies, the salvation of souls, and the building of new visible churches' the whole task of mission? Certainly these are measurable factors of progress in evangelization, but are there not qualitative as well as quantitative criteria that are significant?

2. How far has evangelical concern for personal sanctification obscured the need for congregational sanctification?

3. How far is current enthusiasm for 'development', 'humanization' and the social implications of the gospel a sidetrack from the chief biblical concern of building and perfecting the church?

4. If the verbs used in Acts and the epistles are any guide, the concern of the early church was predominantly directed towards church-planting and perfecting ministries, but is this less important when a national church has been established?

5. When can a national church bridge-head be understood to have penetrated a whole country? How far do ethnic and social sub-cultures also need to be penetrated before a country can be regarded as evangelized?

6. If the task of mission is complete when a national church bridge-head has been established, the 'euthanasia of mission' and temporary moratoria would seem to be valid. However, if church perfecting is equally necessary in both traditional missionary-sending and Third World missionary-receiving coun-

tries, is there not a missionary task still to be completed? Should not euthanasia be regarded as premature until a national church has effectively penetrated the whole of society and until it has been perfected as a credible community of the new humanity?

2 Church and culture

In our first chapter we have been considering the goal of our missionary work; that is, the perfecting of the church. We come now to consider what is a major problem in achieving this goal: namely that the background of the missionary is that of very imperfect Western churches and he has not always found it easy to disentangle his own relative cultural and ecclesiastical values from the unchanging biblical concepts. Thus what one meets in a Third World church is frequently a distressing mixture of second-hand cultural importations syncretized with a subtle blend of indigenous cultural (and often unconsciously religious) values. The universal problem in every country is that many, if not most, of the people involved are not sure what the church is for or where it is going! Thus in borrowing Emil Brunner's telling phrase, 'the misunderstanding of the church', I wish to stress that this universal misunderstanding of the church is further compounded by cultural confusions. As my own missionary experience is predominantly in East Asia, I must inevitably rely heavily upon the writings of others in showing that the same problems are found also in Africa and Latin America. Many of these misunderstandings of the church in the Third World derive in the first place from misunderstandings of the church in Europe and America.

The cultural captivity of the missionary

The missionary's greatest problem is that he has to be born somewhere! He is the product of a particular cultural and ecclesiastical environment, and in many cases knows no other. 'He who never visits thinks his mother is the only cook.'[1] For the missionary's 'church' is inevitably determined by his 'home church' where he has been nurtured, even if he replaces its obvious failings with more idealized concepts. The missionary's mind is full of unconscious and unrecognized ideas about the church which derive not from the Bible but from his own culture. Early missionary training is directed therefore to persuading the missionary candidate that he is the product of a culture. The fish is unaware of being wet until he leaps out of the water and on to strange, dry land. The missionary embarks upon his career wearing cultural contact lenses of which he is almost unaware and which he finds it extremely difficult to remove. And this is just as much a problem for the new Chinese, Japanese, and Korean missions as it is for older American and European ones.

British missionaries find it hard to realize that their 'quiet time' pietism (only possible since Gutenberg made Christians literate), expository preaching, their ABC or 'Four Spiritual Laws' understanding of the gospel, their 'Banner'-waving enthusiasm for reformed theology (whether of 16th century Geneva, 17th century England or 19th century Netherlands) and a multitude of other peculiarities are all to some degree culturally (or subculturally) determined. And even in this list we detect that some aspects of British Christianity have been strongly influenced by European and American culture.

Each nation has a differing concept of the kind of church it is trying to plant. Germans think of great Gothic buildings, ponderous hymns and large tolling bells. The American has a mental image of the church as an efficient organi-

---

[1] A Ganda proverb quoted by J. V. Taylor in *The Primal Vision* (SCM Press, 1969), p.18.

zation with plenty of real estate and a staff of professional specialists. There are more Protestant missionaries from America than any other part of the world and indeed many mission fields are totally dominated by American thinking and cultural patterns. In recent years Americans have consequently faced an increasing wave of criticism and protest, both vociferously from nationals and in a more muted form from fellow missionaries of other nationalities. This attack on 'American cultural imperialism' is perfectly just and fair, and yet in defence of our American brethren it has to be said that it is inevitable. Every missionary brings with him strong cultural presuppositions mixed up with true biblical Christianity. Because there are so many more American missionaries than those of any other nationality, and because American denominations and para-church interdenominational societies have all sought vigorously to propagate themselves around the world and to add the coveted accolade 'International, Inc.' after their names, it is naturally their 'cultural imperialism' which has come under the heaviest fire. But the rest of us need to realize that the ugly European can bring just as much of his culture with him as does the ugly American. Strong cultures like the Japanese, Korean and Chinese are likely to export *at least* as much of their own cultural Christianity as the Americans have done. Indeed all the indications are that they will find it even harder than the Americans to disentangle their own cultural accretions.

René Padilla has exposed the problem for us as it appears in Latin America:[2]

Today, however, there is another form of 'culture Christianity' that has come to dominate the world scene – the 'American Way of Life'. This phenomenon is described by a North American Christian writer in these terms, 'A major source of

    [2] René Padilla, 'Evangelism and the World', *LTEHHV*, pp. 125–126, quoting David O. Moberg, *The Great Reversal* (Scripture Union, 1973), p.42.

the rigid equation of socio-political conservatism with evangelicalism is conformity with the world. We have equated "Americanism" with Christianity to such an extent that we are tempted to believe that people in other cultures must adopt American institutional patterns when they are converted. We are led through natural psychological processes to an unconscious belief that the essence of our American way of life is basically, if not entirely, Christian.' This equation in the United States ensures the presence of a number of middle class whites in the church. But the price the church has had to pay for quantity is to forfeit its prophetic role in society. . . .

It is not surprising that at least in Latin America today the evangelist often has to face innumerable prejudices that reflect the identification of Americanism with the Gospel in the minds of his listeners. The image of a Christian that has been projected by some forms of United States Christianity is that of a successful businessman who has found the formula of happiness, a formula he wants to share with others freely. The basic problem is that, in a market of 'free consumers' of religion in which the church has no possibility of maintaining its monopoly of religion, this Christianity has resorted to reducing its message to a minimum in order to make all men *want* to become Christians. The Gospel thus becomes a type of merchandise, the acquisition of which guarantees to the consumer the highest values – *success* in life and personal *happiness* now and for ever. The act of 'accepting Christ' is the means to reach the ideal of the 'good life' at no cost. The Cross has lost its offence since it simply points to the sacrifice of Jesus Christ for us but it is not a call to discipleship. The God of this type of Christianity is the God of 'cheap grace'.

But American Christians, though their influence may be the most far-reaching, are not the only ones who fall into this trap of *confusing Scripture and culture*. The important general principle behind this particular example is that 'the church must be delivered from anything and everything in its culture that would prevent it from being faithful to the Lord in the fulfilment of its mission within and beyond its own culture. The big question that we Christians always have to ask ourselves with regard to our culture is "Which elements of it should be retained and utilized and which ones should go for the sake of the Gospel?" '³

This is not merely Third World 'sour grapes', a particular Latin American hang-up. One of the most articulate critics has been Jacques Ellul, a Frenchman. He accuses much missionary enterprise of the 'technological mentality' which sees efficiency as the absolute criterion for success, 'the systemization of methods and resources to obtain pre-established results'.⁴ The ultimate corrective becomes not a more biblical gospel, a more faithful church, but a better *strategy*. Yet this is hardly the picture we are given of the New Testament church.

There is another deep-seated problem shared with Americans by British missionaries and indeed all who use English translations of the Bible. They face a cultural translation difficulty in that standard English does not provide any clear differentiation between the second person singular and plural. The *individualistic mind-set of the Anglo-Saxon world* therefore tends to read the New Testament as though it is all addressed to individuals even though it is perfectly clear in Greek, or Chinese, or Japanese or any decent language, that the word 'you' is in the plural and refers to the congregation as a whole. This produces the comic anomaly of the solitary Christian soldier marching out in his Christian armour to engage in single combat with the enemy. No Roman soldier would ever have been so foolhardy and the passage is properly a plural one – 'For *we* wrestle not . . .' (Eph. 6:12, AV). This individualism produces other distortions, so that the church is seen primarily as a means of grace to help the individual 'get saved'. We tend to 'build up' individuals,

³ *Ibid.*, p.136.
⁴ *Ibid.*, p.139.

whereas in the New Testament that phraseology is used primarily for the building up of congregations.

William Smalley has identified the problem as that of the *differentiation of the cultural from the supercultural.* The Christian message of God's reconciling the world to himself, and the faith this gospel produces, are supercultural; but the medium through which the message is communicated and the way in which faith is worked out in individual lives are inevitably moulded by cultural habits and values. The temptation for the missionary is to strive for, and approve of, the changes which will make the people more like himself. Yet if he really believes in the 'indigenous principle' he will yearn for those changes which, under the guidance of the Holy Spirit, meet the needs and fulfil the meanings of that particular society. It is precisely the same tension faced in Jerusalem by the first-century Judaizers who 'saw Greek Christianity through Hebrew eyes'.[5]

Even where intentions are the best, it is easy to use non-indigenous means ostensibly to secure indigenous ends. The story is told of a group of missionaries who, anxious to 'found' a self-supporting church, first established a constitutional committee of three tribesmen and two missionaries. Up till this point the tribesmen had not known that they wanted a constitution and, naturally enough, had no idea what it should include. Consequently, the resulting document was a replica of the denominational constitution of the mission body. The very existence of the constitution seemed entirely irrelevant to the church and to the surrounding community.[6]

The missionary, of course, is not the sole or even the most influential agent of Western cultural infiltration. The influence of Western culture is being felt throughout the

---

[5] William A. Smalley, 'Cultural Implications of an Indigenous Church', in William A. Smalley (ed.), *Readings in Missionary Anthropology* (William Carey Library, Pasadena, 1974), pp.150–152.

[6] *Ibid.*, p.154.

world as a result of commercial activity and mass communication. This is the direction of most cultural change, and some degree of change is inevitable. Each group, then, will develop its own synthesis between the old and the new.

Even our Western mission theories about indigenizing are not immune to cultural interpretation. The basic aim for an indigenous church has always been its independence in matters administrative, financial and evangelistic: self-government, self-support and self-propagation. But Smalley warns us:

> I very strongly suspect that the three 'selfs' are really projections of our American value systems into the idealization of the Church, that they are in their very nature Western concepts based on Western ideas of individualism and power. By forcing them on other people we may at times be making it impossible for a truly indigenous pattern to develop. *We have been Westernizing with all our talk of indigenizing.*[7]

Some missionaries remain totally unconscious of their cultural preconceptions. The problem is rendered more difficult as the majority of missionaries are still native speakers of a European language, tending to work directly from their own language to the indigenous language, and only to a limited extent from the original languages of the Bible. The possibility of a double distortion is thus increased.

Denominationalism

Denominationalism may be regarded as an aspect of the missionary's culture which he is importing with him. There can be few people who will argue seriously that denominationalism is a part of apostolic Christianity. The missionary's denominational background is an accident, sometimes a very local accident, of local church history. Our historical denominations are the product of local

[7] *Ibid.*, p.150, my italics.

historical situations and, humanly speaking, they may be regarded as accidents permitted in the providence of God. If Queen Elizabeth I had not interfered with Parliament's decision to become Presbyterian there might never have come into existence what Malcolm Muggeridge calls 'that curious body' and Sellars and Yeatman 'a good thing', the Church of England. If that same body had been other than it was in the eighteenth century it might not have been necessary for those who wished to be 'methodical' in their religion to form a separate Methodist Church association. If things had been other than they were in the Church of Ireland when John Nelson Darby was one of its ministers, then the Christian Brethren either would not exist as we know them today or would have had an exceedingly different history. Even a church which claims to be founded on 'New Testament principles' is the product of a particular historical situation in a particular country.

Our denominationalism is a cultural by-product, the 'splintered fragments of Western cultural history'.[8] Why else do we find Southern Baptists in North Japan? They are clearly a product of American church history. And how can a Singaporean be an Anglican by conviction? 'What is the body into which I am inviting this man? At the present time the answer has to be 'one of the several hundred bodies into which, in the course of the cultural religious history of the West, the church of God has been divided.'[9]

We can only agree with J. G. Davies when he says that

> (The Protestant) sees the church as the dismembered body of Christ, fragmented into many denominations, some of which uphold different and, indeed, contradictory doctrines. When he speaks of planting the church, he can only mean the planting of denominations. This immediately reduces such

[8] Lesslie Newbigin, *A Faith for This One World?* (SCM Press, 1961), p.124.
[9] *Ibid.*, p.124.

a definition of mission to well nigh an absurdity, as it would mean the increase of Methodists, Lutherans *etc.*. Can it seriously be maintained that this is God's purpose for the world? Is God's primary concern the multiplication of Congregationalists, Presbyterians and the like?[10]

It can, of course, be argued that the multiplication and competition of denominations has encouraged church growth, but the point here is that denominations are not of any universal or eternal value, but rather cultural by-products of local church history, and interdenominational missionary societies aim at carrying out missionary work either by planting new congregations without attaching them to any particular denominational tradition or setting themselves free to co-operate with a variety of indigenous churches which are already attached to existing denominational traditions. Writing in Malaysia, where all the Western denominations, while claiming indigenous goals, yet have their different and distinct congregations, the Rev. George Hood comments:

Most of us are not only members of denominational bodies in this country, but through the international confessional bodies to which our denominations belong have inherited and have become attached to various traditions. While we may recognize our indebtedness to this tradition whichever it may be and the fact that it has been one of the means through which the gospel has been preached in Malaysia, and thereby churches have come into existence, can we claim that Presbyterian, Methodist, Anglican, Lutheran, Brethren, Baptist churches or any of those other bodies which hide their even more exclusive denominationalism under apparently non-denominational titles, can ever as such be truly indigenous, a natural growth? Is it not more likely that in the process of becoming more indigenous, the changes required in each will be so great and far-reaching that the present areas of difference between them will be dwarfed into insignificance? If all

[10] J. G. Davies, 'Church Growth: a Critique', *IRM*, July 1968.

44

these bodies are genuinely concerned to be truly Malaysian, will they not find that they are treading similar paths, and that the issues with which they are faced are so great that they will be driven to learn from each other? ... I find it difficult, if not impossible, to image a truly Malaysian form of Presbyterianism, Methodism, Anglicanism *etc.* It seems more likely that as the various churches travel further along the road to becoming indigenous, they would become less denominational.[11]

There is no doubt that in many missionary situations denominationalism often causes quite unnecessary proliferation of and competition between institutions, many of which are either a heavy financial burden on the indigenous churches or still require financial assistance from the founding mission or parent denomination. In Africa there are usually several denominations working with each language group. Essential biblical teaching should be an unchanging common factor for all denominations. But in practice denominational doctrinal matters and church membership requirements have been placed on a level with these. So there has been duplication of effort in evangelism and the need for separate training facilities. One African ecumenical writer says forthrightly: 'Denominationalism and its proliferations, then, are the product of human selfishness and weakness. Our church leaders in Kenya, present and past, African and expatriate, have made a mess of the church through inheriting and agreeing to accept divisions, through multiplying divisions and through perpetuating division.'[12]

Denominations need to be seen as a reflection of indigenous culture. Thus the episcopalian organization of the Church of England is the ecclesiastical equivalent of the feudal system. The bishops sit in the House of Lords and some

[11] G. Hood, 'Towards an Indigenous Church', *Ecumenical News*, December 1970.
[12] Prof. J. S. Mbiti, quoted by Byang H. Kato in 'The Gospel, Cultural Context and Religious Syncretism, *LTEHHV*, p.1220.

of them expect to be addressed as 'my Lord'. Presbyterian organization reflects the oligarchic pattern of government found in Geneva and other Swiss city states. Equally, the so-called 'independent church' is a reflection in church organization of rugged American individualism. As we shall see in a later section, existing cultural forms of organization are usually, and as a rule properly, influential in determining church structure. New Testament church organization shows a similar variety in differing cultural situations, as can be discovered by the simple exercise of going through the New Testament letters, church by church, instead of endeavouring artificially to produce one single form of church order.

The cultural captivity of the indigenous Christian

If we poor missionaries were the only problem and the national Christians were entirely without any preconceptions or misconceptions, then there would be no difficulty once the latter were fully in control of their own churches. There are some naïve people who assume that self-support and self-government solve everything. In practice it doesn't even ensure that such churches will be self-propagating. If missionaries have cultural contact lenses, then national believers have cultural ear-filters, rejecting some things they hear as irrelevant or inapplicable. The biggest problem, however, is that some things that are thought to have been learned have in fact been misunderstood. The national Christian is a cultural captive too. He also has to be born somewhere and grow up as the product of a particular cultural and social situation.

The problem is further compounded when the missionary fails not only to recognize his own cultural captivity, but fails to realize that the culture of those amongst whom he will be working will be substantially different from his own, in outward behaviour, thought patterns and concepts. Thus the failure of the English Protestant missionaries in West Africa to recognize the differences between the minds of the Africans and their own, their tendency to regard the African minds as so many jugs, which have only to be emptied of the stuff which is in them and to be refilled with a particular form of doctrine they, the missionaries, are engaged in teaching, is certainly one amongst several causes of the mission failures.[13]

True as that may have been of some, it is also true that there have always been other missionaries who, while children of their own generation, have nonetheless been thoughtful and sensitive and learned from their own and others' mistakes.

The African or Asian observes the missionary foreigner both with curiosity and concern: in some ways he seems so knowledgeable, in others, both ignorant and uncouth. 'Europeans are people who do not greet one another in the street' the African observes.[14] There is an enormous cultural gap to be crossed from both sides. Non-Christians begin by attending meetings in the home of the missionary, hoping to discover what this Christian message is all about. They have never met a real Christian before, let alone a congregation. They still have no image of what a Christian is, still less of what a congregation is meant to be. Gradually as they see the missionary and listen to his teaching they begin to form some kind of concept of the Christian and the church which must almost inevitably to some degree be distorted. As we have already seen, the missionary's own concept is strongly coloured by his cultural presuppositions; what we also need to realize is that the indigenous ears of the national have their own cultural 'filter'. The message received by the autocthonous 'seeker' would not necessarily be the same as the message delivered by the international teacher, even if that message were a complete and balanced presentation of the whole

[13] Mary Kingsley in *The National Review*, March 1896, p.71.
[14] J. V. Taylor, *op. cit.*, p.188.

counsel of God. If the missionary knew what his hearer was thinking he would inevitably blurt out 'I did not mean what you thought I said I meant!' There is thus always a process of selection in which incomprehensible or unacceptable ideas are rejected and others are considerably modified.

In the Baptist church in Zaire only ministers are married in church, leaving others free to follow indigenous custom without interference from biblical morality! Again, only when it was seen that Christianity could be used as the religious basis of rebellion was the faith espoused in any widespread way in Buganda. And even then there remained a strong cultural resistance within the general acceptance.

> Overtly pagan rites continued in secret; baptized and regular church-goers continue to this day the practice of magic and even the priesthood of the old gods. Wailing at funerals and the ceremonies at the declaration of the heir (forbidden to Christians because of their association with the ancestor cult) are still used by them. Christian chiefs are still, in some cases, polygamous.[15]

These problems arise for various reasons. Let us take just three main examples of cultural misunderstanding:

1. BAD TRANSLATION

Ekklēsia is a difficult word to translate into any language. Our English translation 'church' is a confusing term, which may be used for a building, a congregation, an institution, an establishment, sometimes for a whole denomination as well as for the universal church of Christ. Germans are able to distinguish between 'Kirche' (church) and 'Gemeinde' (congregation) and it is certainly a pity that Tyndale's translation of *ekklēsia* was not preferred to that of King James's translators. He used the word 'church' only once, in the phrase 'robbers of heathen

---

[15] F. B. Welbourn, *East African Rebels* (SCM Press, 1961), pp.181–182.

48

churches', and elsewhere translated it as 'congregation'. This would certainly have produced a far more people-centred and a far less building-centred view of what Christianity is all about. It can be seen immediately that in any given cultural situation, the suitability of the words selected is of crucial importance.

How can we express faithfully and accurately a given biblical meaning in terms of another language and culture without altering that meaning? A crucial part of the role of theology in any given language or culture is to express the given truths accurately, and to ensure that the original meaning and understanding are not warped, twisted, diluted, narrowed or broadened, and then to go on expressing biblical content without altering biblical meaning. For example, in Chinese and the related languages Japanese and Korean, the same two characters (pronounced variously *chiao-hue*, *kyoo-kai* or *kyoo-hei*) express the meaning 'teaching association'. This immediately suggests that the church is an intellectual circle, a lecturing association where disciples sit passively in order to be instructed by a professional religious teacher. This glaring 'mistranslation of the church' is widespread throughout East Asia.

2. ANALOGY WITH OTHER RELIGIONS

If Christianity is thought of as a religion alongside other known religions, then it is easy to regard the church buildings as homologous with the mosque, temple or shrine and the Christian minister as the equivalent of the 'imam', priest or 'shaman'. The view of Christianity is shaped by *comparison* with other religions rather than directly by the Bible.

In Japan (as in many other countries) 'religion' is a kind of spectator sport in which a ceremony (*e.g.* a Buddhist funeral or a Shinto wedding) is performed by a trained professional. The laymen are spectators of this ritual performance and they reward the 'expert' accordingly (indeed it is commonly believed that this is why he does it: to gain the reward of money or more altruistically of merit). It thus becomes essential to insist that Christianity is *not* a religion in the way in which religions have been commonly understood in Asia, because Christian faith is not merely a form of cultic performance, but of a participating commitment involving the whole of life.

But if the missionary thinks primarily of instituting a routine of services and/or meetings and always presides over these himself, a mistaken and institutionalized, hierarchical one-man band view of the ministry will automatically come into being, because he is reinforcing the cultural misunderstanding.

3. SIMILARITY TO A KNOWN CONCEPT

Throughout Asia, the religious 'teacher' is very much respected. In India, there is the 'guru' and his disciples, derived from Buddhism and Hinduism, in Japan there is the 'sensei' and his disciples, derived from Confucianism and Zen Buddhism. I am told that in South India the word 'guru' is used for ministers, while in Japan the word 'sensei' is a common expression of respect for the Christian minister. This tends to mean that Christian ministry in relation to the congregation at large is defined not by biblical principles but by Buddhist or Confucian ones. In Japan when you join a 'teaching association' you submit yourself to the 'teacher' and do what he tells you. Both in India and Japan it is the minister's responsibility to arrange marriages for Christian young men and women in a congregation. The minister *expects* to be consulted in such matters and would be offended if he were not involved. Instead of many interweaving connections between brethren, the church may be pictured as a wheel, with the teacher as the hub and the believers as the spokes. Even if you move from your original home you will try not to change your church and will commute long distances across a city in order to continue to sit under the ministry of your own 'teacher'. If you move still further away, you may stop attending any local church at all; even if you do attend another one, you will probably not transfer membership and will continue to send your offerings to your original teacher. The concept of the church is thus extraordinarily weakened. Instead of joining an international body of Christians, you become one of a small circle of disciples attached to a particular teacher. There are several unfortunate consequences of this:

a. It produces a congregation of passive spectators.

b. It promotes an authoritarian view of the ministry.

c. It denies the priesthood of all believers by producing a hierarchical system, with a clerical class of teachers and a lower class of laymen.

d. Church growth is restricted. Only a limited number of spokes can be inserted into one hub and if one man is to accept pastoral responsibility for everybody, the church will not grow beyond a certain size.

e. Church growth is also hindered, for one teacher cannot have two circles of disciples and so there is a reluctance to multiply congregations.

f. If a Christian quarrels with his teacher, he will not only have to leave his local 'teaching association' but probably will leave the church of Christ altogether.

An Indian writer actually advocating the adaptation of the idea of the guru to Christian theological training describes the dangers of guru-ism as follows: '. . . authoritarianism in the guru, "fan-ism" in the followers, and sectarianism in both . . . The guru has no colleagues who can keep him in his place.'[16] The underlying assumptions are quite alarming, for the teaching in the *Bhagavad Gita* is that the guru is the supreme godhead itself in visible form. The disciple is to have the same devotion to his guru as he has to his god. The guru, then, is seen in Hinduism as an incarnation of the divine. This would seem to be a rather extreme form of clericalism by any

[16] Vishal Mangalwadi, 'The Guru and Christian Training', *Asia Theological News*, July 1977.

standards! It has certainly travelled a very long way from the New Testament.

The distribution of the word *mathētēs* (disciple) in the New Testament is instructive. The Pharisees and all religious teachers of that period had disciples. John the Baptist and Jesus of Nazareth had disciples. Interestingly, although James and John, Peter and Andrew had been disciples of John the Baptist before becoming disciples of Jesus, they are never said to have had disciples of their own. Nor had Saul of Tarsus once he became a Christian teacher, though he 'sat at the feet' (*i.e.* been a disciple) of Gamaliel and as a Pharisee and a member of the Sanhedrin had had disciples of his own (Acts 9:25). In Acts the word disciple becomes a synonym for Christian, in other words a disciple of Jesus. Paul does not use the word once in his epistles, even for his protegé Timothy whom he regards as his 'true son in the faith'.

We are face to face with a common missionary problem. *How can we accommodate existing concepts and use existing words in a culture without distorting biblical meaning and understanding?*

Indigenization and contextualization

A whole magazine is now being devoted to the subject of contextualization. We can only touch briefly on it here. It is, however, precisely this problem we have been outlining: that *both the missionary and his indigenous hearers are receiving the gospel within a particular cultural context.* Byang Kato defines contextualization as 'making concepts or ideals relevant in a given situation. In reference to Christian practices, it is an effort to express the *never* changing Word of God in *ever* changing modes of relevance. Since the gospel message is inspired but the mode of its expression is not, contextualization of the modes of expression is not only right but necessary.'[17]

As we have seen, while it is by no means universally

[17] Byang Kato, 'The Gospel, Cultural Context and Religious Syncretism', *LTEHHV*, p.1217, my italics.

the case, examples can be found where missionaries have been totally insensitive culturally.

It is bad enough that religious pictures, films and filmstrips should have almost universally shown a white Christ, child of a white mother, master of white disciples; that he should be worshipped almost exclusively with European music set to European hymns, sung by clergy and people wearing European dress in buildings of an archaic European style; that the form of worship should bear almost no relation to traditional African ritual nor the contents of the prayers to contemporary African life.[18]

How ludicrous it is, then, that present congregations of the Anglican church in Africa should still be praying by name for members of the British royal family but not for their own chiefs or political leaders. In contrast to this wholesale importation of alien context one delights in this exposition of much in the New Testament which is calculated to appeal to the African.

The African reading the Bible is glad to find a civilization which marches to the same rythmn as his own. No obsession with efficiency. But life as it unfolds is quite simple in its tragedy, its hopes, its slow rhythm, its cruelties too. Christ walking through the dust from one village to the next, drinking water from the wells, delighting in the movement of the sower, the radiance of the setting sun, the flowers of the field, talking at great length to the crowds – in this we find reflected the black innocence, the irresponsibility of Africa, her timeless existence, her freedom. Christ had no watch and the events of his life are rarely fastened to any date. Westerners strive to map out with some historical guideposts the life of Christ – such is the obsession of the statisticians![19]

It is not surprising, as Byang Kato ably demonstrates,

[18] J. V. Taylor, op. cit., p.13.
[19] J. Claude Bajeux, 'Mentalité noire et mentalité biblique', in Prêtres Noirs, p.60, quoted by Taylor in The Primal Vision, p.24.

that a very strong biblical case can be made for such cultural adaptation:

> The New Testament has given us the pattern for cultural adaptations. The incarnation itself is a form of contextualization. The Son of God descended to pitch his tent among us to make it possible for us to be redeemed. (John 1:14) . . . (This) should motivate us to make the Gospel relevant in every situation everywhere as long as the Gospel is not compromised.[20]

And no compromise will necessarily result from accommodating to indigenous patterns of liturgy, dress, language and music.

The outstanding example of indigenization and contextualization is the wonderfully enlightened decision by Jewish Christians at the Council of Jerusalem that Gentile converts to Christianity were not to be expected to become converts to Jewish culture as well. They were not expected to keep the Jewish ceremonial law but were asked to abstain from fornication, from food offered to idols and from blood.

> The Church, unfortunately, has too often retreated from the bold position of the Council of Jersualem and demanded of its converts some cultural equivalent of circumcision. It is sufficient to mention three such demands – monogamy, teetotalism, and actually, in some areas, uncircumcision – for most of us to rally, as modern Judaizers in defence of the Law. We expect the peasant to opt out of the ancient solidarities of family and tribe and to become individualized, so as to make those personal choices and separations of himself from the mass which we find central to the Christian experience. And, if he is not ready to capitulate, we wait for the forces of change and disruption to break down his defences. They are doing so with grim efficiency, but can we be so confident that they are God's allies?"[21]

[20] Kato, *art. cit.*, *LTEHHV*, p.1217.
[21] J. V. Taylor, *op. cit.*, p.106

This, however, is a very complex problem. Certainly polygamy is found in the Old Testament and though forbidden to kings is practised both by patriarchs and kings; although in the New Testament the Lord Jesus emphatically asserts monogamy as the intended pattern. Thus, as Kato says, the African Christian is to make Christianity culturally relevant without destroying its ever-abiding message. Aspects of African culture should be retained unless and until they are recognized to be unbiblical. To insist on renouncing local culture erects another barrier to the gospel unless it is specifically unbiblical. We notice that Paul (1 Cor. 9:19–23) was ready to become a Jew to the Jews and a Gentile to the Gentiles.

The danger of cultural imperialism is that it produces its own backlash and counter-reaction. Thus in many parts of Africa particularly, there is a reversion to cultural practices which are part of the old paganism, as an over-reaction against the previous wholesale importation of alien cultural practice. In the colonial era all forms of African culture were suppressed and despised, even in the church. The unfavourable comparison was always made with the political power and technical advancement of the West. With the coming of independence, forces of political liberation have also played a great part in bringing African traditional dances back into public entertainment and securing a world-wide market for African handicrafts. As usual, of course, some people want to take this too far and Kato tells us of the African anthropologist who considers that as the Christian teaching on sex confined to marriage is Western, so it must be rejected by the African.

At a theological consultation held in Singapore in June 1970, a Korean scholar suggested that the task of theology is not so much to indigenize the gospel as to *de-indigenize* it. Those who hear the missionaries wear their own cultural ear filters and will automatically indigenize the gospel in terms of their own thought patterns, culture and customs. Indigenization is inevitable, subconscious and difficult to detect. This more subtle kind of secret and unconscious indigenization is the most dangerous and the hardest to correct. It is very difficult for the foreigner to answer the statement 'This is our African way' or 'This is the way we Japanese think'. It is ironical because the foreigner finds it easier to detect distortions and deviations in another culture than he does in his own. In one sense, as the only person understanding his own culture, the national is always right. For the same reason he finds it most difficult to recognize when he is wrong. An African or an Indian is far more alert to discerning the distortions of Anglo-Saxon Christianity than an Englishman or an American would be. We all rejoice in the remarkable church growth experienced in Korea and the wonderful way in which that church has stood against persecution first by the Japanese and then by the communists. At the same time, we are curious to know why it is that Korean Christians so often say to their pastors 'Pray for me, pastor', and why there is quite so much emphasis upon paying money to the church. Certainly, in the old days the shaman would be expected to intercede with God on behalf of the people and would expect to be paid for his services. Is there any relationship between the old Buddhist customs of praying early in the morning and retiring for prayer retreat to the mountains, and the present custom in nearly all Korean churches of having an early morning prayer meeting every day?

To me, one of the most interesting informal sessions at the Lausanne Congress was a small meeting of the Latin American theological fraternity who invited a young Korean scholar studying in Britain, Seiyoon Kim, to address them. He was so bold as to speak about Latin American theology. 'If we are honest,' he said, 'we must admit that this enthusiasm for indigenous theology is largely emotional!' He certainly riveted the attention of his hearers. 'This enthusiasm' he said, 'is largely an over-reaction to your Big Brother in North America. There is no denying that he has added cultural distortions of his own to biblical Christianity. But then all of us are in danger of doing the same thing and distorting the gospel because of our determination to indigenize it.' He urged them to get back to the basic exegetical task of discovering what the Bible says and what the Bible means in our own culture.

Indigenization of form
Although we are clear that biblical content must not be tampered with, we are also clear that forms can and should be indigenized.

1. MUSIC

All over Africa and Asia Christians are singing badly translated Western hymns to the familiar Western tunes. As somebody amusingly commented, 'Africans sing in a minor key. After conversion they sing in a major key. This is only after patient and sustained teaching!'[22] Some of the older Christians in India apparently do not like singing hymns to traditional Indian tunes and so sing the Western ones, even though these are not always recognizable because Indians are unfamiliar with the diatonic scale. But we cannot entirely blame the missionary. Only a few musically gifted missionaries could produce a new hymn tune in diatonic music with meaningful English words. Very few, if any, could be expected to produce pentatonic music, still less write a good hymn in another language. The responsibility for producing new music must depend upon the national church.

One of the very thrilling things in South Thailand in the Malay-speaking church is that the missionaries do not seem to have translated any Western hymns, and the small congregation sings verses of the Bible in their own indigenous music which sounds uncommonly like the call from the minaret with which all are familiar. The musical *form* is national, but the *content* is thoroughly biblical. With

[22] *LTEHHV*, p.1236.

this we may contrast the amusing American habit of importing both a piano and an organ as the only proper way of accompanying a singing congregation!

A pastor from Cuba commenting on the withdrawal of missionaries said, 'Many North American ways of doing things have disappeared. Church services are freer and more spontaneous. Our light and senseless gospel choruses have been abandoned. Singing is predominantly Latin American!'[23] And Mr. Ben Dyrit, the Vice-Principal of the Philippines Missionary Institute commented, 'Whenever I pass a Roman Catholic service and hear the music, all my Filipino and Spanish blood responds. How shallow is our Protestant worship! What have we got? A song leader standing out in front and shouting "Let's all sing. . . ."!'

One of the most amusing situations at the Lausanne World Congress arose from the very strong and perfectly justifiable criticism of 'missionary imperialism' in some of the magnificent Latin American contributions to the Congress already discussed. Although the vast majority of the delegates approved heartily of these criticisms almost a week passed before it occurred to anybody that somebody besides Cliff Barrows could lead the singing. A Chinese who replaced him led the singing in a manner indistinguishable from Cliff Barrows!

It is, however, possible to go overboard in an endeavour to indigenize one's music. In Africa, for instance, the educated young Christians, cut off from their traditional music over several generations, are much more at home composing for the guitar than the drums and flutes. Present-day Africans use jazz and other musical forms to produce contemporary music that is original and peculiarly their own. As one African put it: 'Must they go back to drums and other rattles to be African?'[24] The important

[23] Quoted by Wolf Hansen in *EMQ*.
[24] John Mpaayei, *LTEHHV*, p.1229.

factor is the opportunity to create new forms of worship particularly suited to cultural needs.

2. CHURCH SERVICES

Mr Ben Dyrit points out that for some reason, presumably initially unconscious missionary influence, morning services are normally held at 10.30 a.m. in Protestant Filipino churches. In the tropics, however, this is far too close to lunch time and by the time the sermon starts everybody is far too sleepy and hungry to concentrate. It was not that the missionary deliberately determined to force a Western pattern on the people to whom he went, but merely that he followed his normal custom. Indigenization ought probably to mean moving morning services to 7 or 8 a.m., in the cool of the day when people are still fresh and can think clearly. It is perhaps significant that in Singapore, Brethren assemblies which have long been independent of foreign missionary control usually 'break bread' at 8 a.m.

Round the world, the pattern of the hymn sandwich with the sermon between the last two hymns seems to have been passed on by missionaries. In the English-speaking world, that habit of having the sermon at the end arises from the period when the Puritans who had been under the influence of the Reformers in Strasburg and Geneva returned to England after the death of Queen Mary. According to law the 'form in the said book prescribed' (the *Book of Common Prayer*) had to be read while wearing the white surplice, also prescribed by law. Only when this had been completed would the Protestant preacher don a black Geneva gown in order to preach. There are still some churches in Britain that maintain this practice of gown-changing! While the origins of the custom have been forgotten, the practice of retaining the sermon at the end (except in the Anglican communion service) proves stubbornly difficult to alter. Churches which pride themselves on being non-conformist still quite rigidly have the sermon at the end even though there are good arguments for having it much earlier. Interestingly, in Islam the sermon or exposition of the Koran precedes the period of worship. There is a lot to be said in non-conformist patterns for allowing worship to arise naturally and spontaneously out of a response to the Word of God, rather than preceding the sermon with 'preliminaries', often a poor substitute for genuine worship. All of us are cultural captives when asked to lead a Christian service of worship.

3. THEOLOGICAL EDUCATION

The forms of theological education are peculiarly fossilized. Our theological colleges find their origin in the monastic tradition which preceded the Reformation. Thus, traditionally, theological education has always tended to be monastic and to withdraw men from the world to train them. The new patterns of theological education by extension are beginning to break this inherited mould.

Western theological training has also tended to be content-orientated rather than goal-orientated. People are dropped into the time-honoured theological machine and emerge at the other end at so many Revs per annum without hard questions being asked as to whether the men have been prepared properly for what they are intended to be able to perform. Our education has also been much more academic than pedagogic and the individual is examined upon what he knows rather than upon what he is able to teach and communicate effectively to others. There is far more stress upon cognitive input (knowing) rather than upon psycho-motor skills (doing) and behavioural change (being). Training for the ministry consists almost entirely of pouring large cognitive doses into the minds of the students, as though they were so many academic jugs, without very much reference to the usefulness or otherwise of all that information when they proceed into the normal life of the ministry.

There seems little point in teaching church history in the traditional order from AD 30 to the present day, to people who know nothing of the Europe of the Renaissance and the Reformation, still less of ancient Greece and Rome. It is not that church history should not be taught but that the missionary's old theological college church history notes now have to be entirely rethought and recast. They must be made relevant to people whose own church history may stretch back less than 100 years and who are more likely to be interested in the church history of neighbouring Asian countries and conceivably in the origins of the founding missionary bodies than those aspects of church history which have interested us in the West.

Again, in considering a curriculum, the subject of 'homiletics' as it is generally taught is a Western cultural form which majors on the academic apprehension of truth, rather than insistence upon obedience and performance. The Bible consists of short, snappy statements demanding human obedience. We have learned 'how to expound', these, and 'expounding' usually means expanding a simple statement to last anything from twenty to forty minutes.

Once one has learned the technique, one can even do it with nursery rhymes: 'Three blind mice'. You notice their number, their condition and their kind. Your attention is particularly directed to their mode of locomotion. 'See *how* they run.' You can certainly have some fun with that!

Please don't misunderstand me. I am strongly in favour of expository preaching (as opposed to either impository or juxtapository preaching) but our Western approach to 'the sermon' is not always based on sound educational principles. We are not interested merely in occupying twenty or thirty minutes of the congregation's time. The aim of preaching is to change men's lives. Western congregations have long since discovered that it makes no difference whether you take any notice or not: nobody will ever check up on you! Japanese comment that Western homiletics seems to convey a tremendous amount of information. 'We Japanese', they say, 'don't only want to know a doctrine, we want to feel it, we want to experience it, we want to emote over it!' The whole manner of preaching sermons has to be rethought in terms of the new culture.

I have spent some time on this for I want us to see the extent to which our cultural assumptions need to be challenged when we move as missionaries into a new environment. It is a stimulating, mind-blowing experience. The whole practice of church life and worship now needs to be rethought from biblical principles. It is an exciting and challenging adventure.

4. CHURCH GOVERNMENT

Are we to regard church government as part of the unchanging biblical content or as a culturally alterable form? We have already seen that a good deal of church order may be culturally determined. It does seem natural that the forms of authority, organization and leadership already indigenous in a society should be reflected in the organizational structures of the Christian church.

Although it is possible to be dogmatic about church government based on bishops, priests and deacons on the one hand, and on ministers, elders and deacons on the other, the problem presented by these different views arises because we seek artificially to force out of Scripture a single uniform 'doctrine of the ministry', when it is dubious that such ever existed. The New Testament seems much more interested in the moral character and behaviour and in the spiritual gifts of overseers, elders and deacons than it does in providing any structure for their relationships or even job descriptions of their respective responsibilities. If we study the New Testament book by book, we discover a remarkable cultural diversity in patterns of leadership. Jewish synagogues were presided over by elders, and it is not surprising therefore that the predominantly Jewish church in Jerusalem was presided over by *presbuteroi*. By contrast, many Gentile societies had superintendents and this term *episkopoi* is used of the Ephesian elders (Acts 20:28), and in writing to Timothy working in Ephesus (1 Tim. 3:1). There is no mention of elders in Philippi, only of bishops and deacons. In Rome and Thessalonica there is no mention of bishops or elders but of *proistamenoi*, that is 'those who are over you', or those who preside. In Corinthians there is no mention of elders or overseers but rather of *kubernēsis* (related to the word *kubernētēs*, steersman) translated 'administration'. The letter to the Hebrews uses none of these expressions but introduces yet another term, *hēgoumenoi*, leaders (Heb. 13:7, 17, 24), an expression also reflected in the description of Silas and Judas Barsabbas as 'leading men among the brethren' (Acts 15:22). The only general conclusion is that, while there is always officially recognized authority and leadership which is to be respected and obeyed, the actual titles used and the mode of organization are quite indifferent.

Let me give an amusing illustration from my own experience. In the north Japan field of the OMF the early missionaries decided that they would plant independent autonomous congregations practising believer's baptism. As these independent autonomous churches came into existence, they began to organize summer conferences, evangelistic radio broadcasts and other joint activities. Accordingly each congregation sent two representatives to an Evangelical Church Association (ECA) which made decisions in such matters on behalf of all the churches. Almost imperceptibly, these churches founded on a congregational pattern became presbyterian and initiated a presbytery or synod. The process, however, was not yet complete. Both missionaries and national Christians felt that a Bible college was needed to train men for full-time ministry. In the Confucian social pattern in Japan, the principal of the Bible school occupied a special position as the original teacher of the younger teachers in the different congregations. If they had a problem, what was more natural but to go back to him for help and advice?

Indeed, if they had a problem and did not go to him, then the principal would feel it his duty to go to them because in everyone's eyes he was responsible for their teaching and conduct. Was he not their teacher? You will appreciate that we now have a bishop! While the ECA is never called a presbytery nor the principal called a bishop, as far as the structure goes it already amounts virtually to this. Every denomination in Japan, whether called Episcopalian or Presbyterian, Independent or even Brethren, tends to approximate to a cultural norm which relates to the ordinary social pattern of leadership in the country as a whole.

There are particular missionary problems in Thailand where nearly every minister is independently supported, either through his own private means and resources or by the labour of his wife. In Thai culture it is unthinkable that one should be taught by somebody whom one employs. It thus seems that some pattern of ministry must be found where ministers will not be financially supported by the congregations they teach. One is reminded that Jewish rabbis were apparently not remunerated for their teaching but supported themselves by working with their hands. The apostle Paul acted fully in this tradition when he refused to be supported by the church with which he was working and instead provided for himself as a leather worker using the goatskins from his native Cilicia.

Scripture thus seems to allow a very considerable degree of flexibility in church order, provided there is order. It seems much wiser, therefore, for missionaries to allow nationals to arrive at their own pattern of church order, rather than arbitrarily to impose an alien pattern from their own previous experience.[25] Provided it is not specifically anti-scriptural it would seem that any pattern

[25] In the light of this kind of biblical thinking it is almost laughable to think that, for example, 'Episcopalian ordination' in the so-called Lambeth Quadrilateral was made one of the essential conditions for church union.

of organization which is socially acceptable would be in accord with the flexibility and variety of structures found within the New Testament.

Cultural hindrances to church growth

1. THE MAJOR CULTURAL BLOCS

In any country where the overwhelming majority of the population are adherents to a non-Christian religion, the individual's opportunity of making any meaningful response to Christianity is seriously curtailed. He is unlikely to hear a coherent explanation of the content of Christianity through any of the major media, although one hopes it would be possible for him to get hold of a New Testament and other Christian literature (though in the absence of Christian bookshops and Christian publishers this cannot necessarily be assumed). Even if there is a faint possibility of hearing the Christian gospel in a monolithic society hostile to Christianity, however, it is extremely difficult for an individual to make an independent decision to become a Christian. Though adherence to the majority religion may be nominal, hostility immediately emerges if anybody tries to opt out of it. This is particularly true of Muslim countries.

The Universal Declaration of Human Rights was proclaimed by the United Nations on 10th December 1948. Article 18 reads as follows:

> Everyone has the right to freedom of thought, conscience and religion; this right includes freedom to change his religion or belief, and freedom either alone or in community with others and in public or private to manifest his religion or belief in teaching, practice, worship or observance.

This part of the Declaration is being flagrantly violated by a number of member nations who have not ratified it in their national parliaments. In certain Muslim countries there exists the freedom to change one's religion *to* Islam, but there is no genuine freedom for the individual to turn *from* Islam to another religion. Indeed the Shariah (Muslim Law) prescribes death for such a person. It is time that enthusiasts for human rights turned their attention to this particular denial of human freedom.

As Christians we must insist that genuine religious freedom allows an individual not only to hold his own personal beliefs, but also to propagate them and to change his convictions if he so chooses: either from Christianity to another religion or from another religion to Christian faith. It is understood that governments are concerned about the exercise of public order and anxious to prevent demonstrations of hostility by adherents of the majority religion against those of minority religions. At the same time, Christians as good citizens must respect the need for maintaining public order and be careful that the manner in which they propagate their faith does not prove deliberately provocative. But even where freedom theoretically exists, in practice it may be severely curtailed because of social pressure. That we 'formerly walked according to the course of this world' (Eph. 2:2) holds true for many people where the course of social pressure is such that it is extremely difficult, if not impossible, publicly to confess adherence to Christ.

Such prejudice is particularly strong in the two other great monotheistic non-Christian faiths whose adherents, together with Christians, call on the God of Abraham, Isaac and Jacob. And for this prejudice the Christian church must accept a great deal of responsibility. The Christian movement was originally entirely a Jewish movement:

> One of the astounding facts of this early history was that the leaders of the movement for Yeshua became convinced that the Gentiles were to be given the opportunity to respond to the message . . . after deliberation, the leaders adopted an open-door policy towards Gentiles. Jews, they decided, are called to a specific task; Gentiles however, are not necessarily called to be Jews. Gentiles could be considered accepted by

God and one with Jews in faith through Yeshua if they followed the basic way of life taught by him. (This is parallel to the Jewish notion that the Noahic covenant was incumbent upon all peoples. Some rabbis did not believe that righteous Gentiles were called to follow all of the Jewish law but only those Noahic principles.) The Council said, in effect, that there could be two wings of the movement of Yeshua – a loyal Jewish wing and a Gentile wing. Each group was to consider the other accepted by God. Neither was to seek to dissolve the other wing into its culture. There could be unity without uniformity; oneness and diversity. Jews were still called to be Jews, but Gentiles were not asked to take upon themselves the whole of Israel's calling as a people.[26]

The tragedy is that while Jewish Christians did not bind Gentiles to their culture and allowed them to develop their Christian faith in terms of their own varied cultures, before many centuries had passed the Christian nations of the world were persecuting the Jews.

Likewise, the prejudice of Islam against Christianity has an historical base.

The acceptability of the Christian message among the Muslims was hindered by ill-will retained from the age of the Crusaders. There was also the fact that Christianity had approached the Muslims almost invariably from a Hellenic base. The Apostle Paul had felt that he should be a Greek to the Greeks, and a Jew to the Jews. He might just as well have suggested that he be a Muslim to the Muslims. It is not beyond reason to suppose that Muslims might become truly believers in Jesus Christ as Saviour and Lord without calling themselves Christians, even as the 'Messianic Jews'. Theoretically then, what was needed, was for the Muslims to become believers without having to abandon their Muslim language and culture.[27]

[26] Daniel C. Juster, *Jewishness and Jesus* (IVP, Illinois, 1977).
[27] Ralph D. Winter, 'The World Christian Movement 1950 – 1975'. An interpreted essay from the Revised Edition of Kenneth Scott Latourette, *A History of Christianity* (Harper and Row, 1975), p.26.

It is almost comical now to remember that even that great missionary to Muslims, Samuel Zwemer, believed that as so many Muslim peoples were then under British rule it was only a matter of time before they abandoned Islam in favour of Christianity.

Compared with monistic, pantheistic and animistic religion, there is so much more common ground between Christians and both Jews and Muslims. All of us are monotheists. Muslims even believe that Jesus will be the one who will come to judge the world. Everything found in the Law and the Prophets we as Christians enthusiastically affirm and accept. Both radical Christian thinking and humility are needed in penitence for the wrong attitudes of 'Christian nations' to Jews and Muslims. The Old Testament contains remarkable prophecies which see Egypt and Assyria sharing faith in the same Lord as Israel (Is. 19:18, 21, 24–25). But the same dedication and commitment which Raymond Lull, Henry Martyn and Samuel Zwemer gave to work among Muslims needs to be found in men and women in this present day and age.

2. SUBCULTURAL BLOCS

In view of the clarity of Christians about some social evils it is remarkable how many have been ready to accept peaceful co-existence with problems of caste and social class.

> Christian missionaries have set their faces against all the patently 'uncivilized' aspects of native culture, whether or not they were strictly forbidden by the Scriptures; they have opposed polygamy, slavery, the payment of the bride-price, initiation ceremonies, dancing, wailing at funerals, and the belief in magic, along with human sacrifice and the exposure of twins, as all being equally repugnant to civilization in which mechanical warfare was a recognized institution.[28]

One of the outstanding problems is that of caste in

[28] Noel P. Mair, *An African People in the Twentieth Century* (Routledge and Kegan Paul, 1934), p.3.

India. Should the Christian church reject caste and become alien or should it accept caste and cease to be Christian? The argument runs on and on. Certainly Scripture says that in Christ 'there is neither bond nor free, neither Jew nor Greek', but it also says 'neither male nor female'. Thus while these differences are not to be regarded as significant in Christ, nobody has suggested that sex difference should be abolished and most people live very happily with it. More recently some have argued that it is easier to evangelize and plant churches of like-minded people by accommodating oneself to the caste structure than by trying to destroy it. The fact remains that these subcultural differences provide a substantial barrier to the progress of the gospel.

> One of the great practical obstacles to Christian work in India was the fact that most Christians there – the main exception being the Syrian tradition – came from the depressed classes, earlier called 'untouchables'. This fact demonstrated to India, more graphically than anything else could have, the phenomenal power of the Christian faith to transform and uplift. It also tended to seal off the Christian movement within certain social classes. A few voices were raised in defence of a deliberate 'second front' into the higher strata of the former caste system. Asked what receptivity there might be for Christianity on the part of the 500 million middle caste peoples of India, one leader suggested that at least 100 million of these people would become Christians if it were possible for them to do so without abandoning their entire social inheritance. Yet many Christians tend to believe that social evils, seemingly perpetuated by the traditional social structures, could be conquered only by displacing these structures. . . . The majority of more than one thousand caste groups constituting at least 80% of the population had as yet no branch of the Christian Church represented within their communities.[29]

Even in very recent years, the fact that Christians

[29] Ralph D. Winter, 'World Christian Movement', p.27.

belonged to different social castes has been a cause of strife and law suits within the Christian churches.

The missionary has to accept social class as a fact of life, and yet his own usefulness stems from the significant fact that as a foreigner he himself is outside the indigenous caste system. The Japanese pastor is a prisoner of a stratified social class system. With the company president or the university professor he must be so busily involved in courteous recognition of the other's status that he may become ineffective as a witness to Christ. Equally the country peasant is too busy giving courteous verbal agreement to everything the religious teacher has to say to be able to accept genuinely the message that the pastor brings. However, one of the advantages of being a Christian missionary is that one is totally outside the class structure. The missionary can witness to a country peasant or the most respected intellectual. He can be brother to a beggar and comrade to a king. This wide spectrum of effectiveness is often forgotten in discussions of the missionary's continued usefulness. Certainly in pioneering situations the foreigner who is outside the social class system is often the more effective evangelist. Applying this to our own society we are only too well aware that a plummy Oxbridge accent on the one hand or a chronic lack of aspirates on the other may result in acceptance or rejection according to the social group. The success of American evangelists in Britain can be at least partly attributed to the fact that in terms of British culture it is impossible to classify them as working, middle or upper class. It may well be that missionaries from abroad could be more effective in certain social strata in this country than indigenous evangelists. In the same way, Christians in some of the castes of India have found it impossible to break out from their social imprisonment to reach those in other classes.

This point needs to be borne in mind when considering the difference between the establishment of an indigenous church as a small bridge-head and the effective penetra-

70

tion of a whole country with the gospel. But if the national church is limited within certain geographical, ethnic or social subcultures it may need the assistance of international missionaries in order to break out of its subcultural bridgehead.

3. ADOPTION OF 'CHRISTIAN' CULTURAL PRACTICES

When Paul urged his converts to be 'imitators of me' he was expressing a fact of life. Foreign missionaries will be imitated whether they like it or not and whether they are good models or not. Sometimes this imitation can be funny. Bishop Stephen Neill told me that for many years the more spiritual Christian ministers in Tinnivelly all sported large moustaches in imitation of the much respected Tom Walker of Tinnivelly. In Ghana, there are Christian speakers who have been taught in Westminster Chapel long enough for them to return to their own country having taken on the accents of Dr Martyn Lloyd-Jones. In Japan, it is noticeable that people with different traditions have different manners of praying: some pray almost in whispers while others seem to feel that they will only be heard if they shout, clap and hiss. The probability is that the innocent mannerisms of early influential missionaries were accepted as the authentic way of praying, so that purely personal idiosyncracies were adopted as part of the culture of Christianity. Sometimes these problems are much more serious. Remembering what autocrats some colonial bishops were, it is not altogether surprising that when the national Christians became bishops they could be even more autocratic than their models.[30] In Africa this autocracy is partly attributable to

---

[30] There was a nice story about Archbishop Clayton of Capetown who 'was a firm believer in democratic government . . . the struggle in him between this belief in democracy and his own will was to last throughout his life, and each had its own triumphs, some of them of high entertainment value, with either a triumphant Clayton obviously embarrassed by his own victoriousness or a defeated Clayton glowering angrily at the stupidity of the democratic will' (Alan Paton, *Apartheid and the Archbishop*, David Philip, 1973).

tribal culture and the authority of the chief reflected in the ecclesiastical sphere.

However, imitation of the foreigner extends beyond his personal idiosyncracies to much in his lifestyle which reflects his total Western cultural orientation rather than his Christian convictions. This is a much more serious matter and raises deep complications. Just as Africans respond collectively *from* their total cultural background, so they respond *to* a total culture. The missionary's message may not be disentangled from his cultural background; they are very closely identified in the African mind. Many features may rightly be classified as British, French or American, but what can be separated for the purpose of study blends together to form the total Christian-Western culture to which the African responds. The problem is compounded by the fact that these identifications have been institutionalized into the African church. So it is now the African church leaders who reject African music and insist on Western wedding dress and receptions, and press for the continued use of the *Book of Common Prayer*.

We shall return to this problem of the total impact of a total culture in our next chapter where we see that much that is offered in Christian aid is the product not so much of Christianity as of Western technology and materialism.

4. ANIMISTIC IDEAS SYNCRETIZED WITH CHRISTIAN FAITH

The cultural tradition in Indonesia may well be described as remarkably rich. The underlying strata are of course animistic. These were overlaid first with Hinduism (still the religion of Bali), then with Buddhism, then with Islam and finally with a thin Christian icing! Schreiner of Wuppertal writes of the Bataks that the persistence of the tribal *adat* has never been challenged at the deeper level. In many churches in Indonesia and Sarawak a dependence on fetishes, charms and folk medicine continues to persist in Christian congregations. It is particularly in times of spiritual revival, such as have occurred in parts of these two countries, that a fresh repentance results in the burning and destruction of such charms and fetishes as well as more modern pin-up pictures. This persistence of animistic ideas can even be found in our own Anglo-Saxon culture. The use of holly, mistletoe and pine trees at Christmas time are remnants of animistic practice. Ideas of holy water and the churching of women quite possibly go back to the druids. Hallowe'en and All Souls are the remains of pagan roots of spirit worship which are remarkably similar to the 'obon' festivals celebrated by Chinese, Koreans and Japanese when the spirits of their departed ancestors are escorted home from the graveyard for a brief visit to their descendants.

Attitude to culture

One of the best statements on this is to be found in the Lausanne Covenant (clause 10 Evangelism and Culture):

> The development of strategy for the world evangelization calls for imaginative pioneering methods. Under God, the result will be the rise of churches deeply rooted in Christ and closely related to their culture. Culture must always be tested and judged by Scripture. Because man is God's creature, some of his culture is rich in beauty and goodness. Because he has fallen, all of it is tainted with sin and some of it is demonic. The Gospel does not presuppose the superiority of any culture to another, but evaluates all cultures according to its own criteria of truth and righteousness, and insists on moral absolutes in every culture. Missions have all too frequently exported with the Gospel an alien culture, and churches have sometimes been in bondage to culture rather than to the Scripture. Christ's evangelists must humbly seek to empty themselves of all but their personal authenticity in order to become the servants of others, and churches must seek to transform and enrich culture, all for the glory of God.[31]

[31] *LTEHHV*, pp.6–7.

This provides a wonderful summary of what we have been trying to say. *The fact of diversity is very important. It is not our responsibility to offer American, German or British Christianity to the world but the message of the lordship of Jesus Christ in its pure biblical form.*

The record is not all negative, though, as Paul Tillich points out: 'The fact that there are new churches in another cultural orbit, developing their independence and resisting the identification of the kingdom of God with any special form of Christianity is perhaps the greatest triumph of Christian missions.'[32]

Tillich also shoots down the liberal notion that missions have the responsibility of amalgamating culture. He points out that this attitude of 19th century liberals resulted merely in the 'primitive' cultures being changed into the 'higher' cultures.

We have already given considerable space to the problem of cultural imperialism, recognizing with the Lausanne Statement the danger that missionaries may export an alien culture packaged up with the gospel. McGavran writes with characteristic energy about this: 'Eurican cultural overhang must be rejected.' And becomes positively euphoric as he looks forward to the coming church:

> The Church stripped of her cultural accretions, alone with her book and obedient to her Lord, is the unchanging core, but her periphery changes. When, for example, by the year 2000 there are 100,000,000 Christians in Africa, we may be sure that the church will appear in many African guises. She will not speak English and French, but a thousand languages. She will be housed in a million village churches. Although thoroughly grounded in a thousand tribes and appearing as lingustic denominations, she will be breaking down the walls of hostility and pressing on to supra-tribal unity. Since the denomination is the form the church takes in the 20th century, her congregations will group themselves into many African

[32] Paul Tillich, 'Mission and World History' in G. H. Anderson (ed.), *The Theology of the Christian Mission* (SCM Press, 1961), p.288.

denominations of many colourful names. Movements to Christian unity will surge through the denominations, and regroupings will appear again and again. The periphery will change; but since these denominations will be local manifestations of the church of Jesus Christ against which the gates of hell will not prevail, the core will not change. And the whole church will multiply exceedingly.[33]

Christianity, as it exploded across the world, displayed a remarkable capacity to become clothed in the language and culture of all peoples accepting it, and at the same time to bind these diverse peoples into fellowship with other Christians in other parts of the world.[34]

Culture then ought not to be seen primarily as a problem or a hindrance to the gospel but as a potential enrichment of it. It is like the rich, spicy garnishing of pickles with a variety of tastes which brings constant, delightful variety to the unchanging, staple, rice-like nourishment of the gospel.

Conclusions

The challenge of culture is a thrilling adventure for the missionary. In learning a new language the whole of one's theology and teaching has to be rethought, as one not only converts it into new words, but finds new illustrations and new ways of conveying the unchanging biblical content. To illustrate, the human face is still normally recognizable from year to year, even though every single molecule of that facial structure will have been replaced by another molecule in the course of the year. If it takes a good mind to teach theology in one's own language, it takes a better one, and provides a greater intellectual challenge, to have to do it in terms of another language and another culture. There is nothing so stimulating to thought, so seminal, so mind-blowing, as having to cross cultural barriers with the gospel. It can be so dull to stay

[33] McGavran, 'Church Growth Strategy Continued', *IRM*, July 1968, p.339.
[34] *Cf.* Ralph Winter, *art. cit.*, p.28.

at home. You can get bogged down in your intellectual ruts. You can become imprisoned in your theological ivory tower and waste a good deal of heat and light on relatively minor issues. If you want to use your life in a worthwhile way, if you want action, then grapple with the problems of communicating Christian truth acceptably to Jews and Muslims and Hindus and Buddhists. *Let us grapple with the problem of what is essential to the content of the Christian faith.* In our own country we may be wrestling with controversies about Scripture and the atonement, biblical hermeneutics and semantics, but in the wider situation one is faced with problems that people here have never thought of and are never likely to think of. The missionary task demands that the Christian worker girds up the loins of his mind to face this fascinating diversity of culture in which the universality of the Christian gospel is to be proclaimed. Dare I hope that your persistence in reading so far with this book displays not merely an academic interest but a passionate sense of involvement and a desire to enter upon the fantastic adventure of cross-cultural mission in the service of our Lord Jesus Christ?

Material for study

William A. Smalley (ed.), *Readings in Missionary Anthropology* (William Carey Library, Pasadena, 1974). See especially two contributions by the editor, 'Cultural Implications of an Indigenous Church' and 'What are Indigenous Churches like?'
Byang H. Kato, 'The Gospel, Cultural Context and Religious Syncretism' *LTEHHV*, pp. 1216ff., and see also the report on the following discussion.
John T. Mpaaye, 'How to Evaluate Cultural Practices by Biblical Standards in Maintaining Cultural Identity in Africa', *LTEHHV*, pp.1229ff.
John V. Taylor, *The Primal Vision* (SCM Press, 1969).
Eugene A. Nida, *Customs, Culture and Christianity* (Tyndale Press, 1963).

Questions for discussion

1. Do you think it possible that there are Anglo-Saxon distortions of and accretions to biblical Christianity in our culture? Why is it difficult to recognize them? Give a list.

2. When does a cultural accretion become a hindrance to the gospel? What clear authority is there for determining this?

3. Jewish Christians at the Council of Jerusalem decided not to force Greek Christians into a Jewish mould, even though this could be justified by Old Testament scripture. Can you think of ways in which missionaries have imposed their own cultural distortions upon indigenous churches?

4. In the light of 1 Corinthians 9:19–23, how far should missionaries accept the language, dress conventions, food regulations and customs of the people they go to win?

5. What are the necessary aspects involved in 'freedom of religion'? How can the Declaration of Human Rights be effectively implemented?

3 The church in the world

One of the most interesting developments in recent years has been a landslide of evangelical thinking around the world and a welcome and fresh restatement of the social implications of the gospel. Twenty years ago there was an extreme polarization between, on the one hand, theological conservatives stressing the vertical relationship between man and God and putting their energies almost exclusively into evangelism, beseeching men to be reconciled to God, and on the other, theological liberals giving themselves to good works and stressing man's horizontal responsibilities towards his less fortunate neighbour. Now we are faced with an entirely different situation. Every congress on evangelism seems ready to go overboard in emphasizing the importance of Christian social involvement, and seems to have achieved a much greater balance between the vertical and the horizontal in proclaiming the importance both of love towards God and love towards one's fellow man. There does not yet seem to have been a corresponding readjustment on the part of theological liberals to the importance of preaching the saving gospel of Christ and him crucified, to the countless millions of lost sheep, astray from God and dead in trespass and sins. Vain efforts are still being made to show that some of the thieves and robbers might be good shepherds in disguise and that the lost sheep are all 'anonymous Christians' without really realizing it!

It is impossible for the evangelist and church planter in Thailand to ignore the social environment of those to whom he preaches. Crop failure from either flood or drought occurs two years in every five. Therefore farmers must borrow from money lenders who may charge as much as 10% per month. At a recent training weekend for lay leaders eleven out of the twelve present admitted to being seriously in debt. Many farmers have only five to ten acres, and some of this may be leased or mortgaged so that a third or a half of the yield has to go to the landlord. Giving up the unequal struggle, many turn to drink. When the existing farm cannot support the parents, what happens if they have eight or ten children? There is little hope of their supporting themselves on the land. They cannot obey the creation ordinance to work, and unemployed young men with little prospect of honest work turn to crime and violence. Missionaries attacked and robbed by such youngsters cannot ignore the underlying causes. Why does the church not grow faster or why is it not more alive both to its evangelistic and social responsibilities? Bad dietary habits and chronic malnutrition slow everybody down, as does parasitic infestation. Children who are undernourished in the early years also lack the intellectual stimulation from torpid mothers. Church growth is directly affected because Christians, like others, do not enjoy full health.

Nor can one blame the Thai government which was wrestling with a Gross National Product per capita income in 1976 of US $380 as against the UK's $4,000 or the United States $7,890. Compare the following figures, all for 1976:

Total public expenditure of Thailand	£1,389 millions
Annual tobacco consumption of UK	£2,741 millions
Annual alcohol consumption of UK	£4,902 millions
Annual defence expenditure of UK	£5,173 millions
Annual cost of NHS of UK	£5,260 millions
Annual education expenditure of UK	£6,840 millions

Britain has a population of 55 million, Thailand 40 million; but Thailand's total public expenditure amounts to only a sixth of what we spend on alcohol and tobacco. Though we as missionaries may have a single eye to planting and perfecting churches, we know that the church is perfected as it goes out together into the world to bring blessing to its non-Christian neighbours.

It is worth noting here the Lausanne Covenant statement on Christian Social Responsibility (clause 5):

> We affirm that God is both the Creator and the Judge of all men. We therefore should share his concern for justice and reconciliation throughout human society and for the liberation of men from every kind of oppression. Because mankind is made in the image of God, every person, regardless of race, religion, color, culture, class, sex or age, has an intrinsic dignity because of which he should be respected and served, not exploited. Here too we express penitence both for our neglect and for having sometimes regarded evangelism and social concern as mutually exclusive. Although reconciliation with man is not reconciliation with God, nor is social action evangelism, nor is political liberation salvation, nevertheless we affirm that evangelism and socio-political involvement are both part of our Christian duty. For both are necessary expressions of our doctrines of God and man, our love for our neighbor and our obedience to Jesus Christ. The message of salvation implies also a message of judgment upon every form of alienation, oppression and discrimination, and we should not be afraid to denounce evil and injustice wherever they exist. When people receive Christ they are born again into his kingdom and must seek not only to exhibit but also to spread its righteousness in the midst of an unrighteous world. The salvation we claim should be transforming us in the totality of our personal and social responsibilities. Faith without works is dead.[1]

There is a wealth of helpful books on this subject and

[1] *LTEHHV*, pp.4–5.

it is not possible to cover all the ground in a brief chapter. However, it is worth first of all reviewing the biblical basis of Christian social involvement particularly as it affects missionary work. Secondly, because the impression has been wrongly given that in the past missions have pursued the salvation of souls but have ignored men's social needs and have been hand in glove with colonial exploitation, it would be useful to say something about the history of missions in social involvement. Thirdly, because it seems to me that many evangelical Christians, having become aware that their earlier understanding of the gospel was one-sided, are now in serious danger of swinging to the opposite extreme, I would like to show that naïve enthusiasm for social involvement is not without its dangers in relation to the modern missionary movement. In the face of protest, particularly from the Islamic world, against Christians using medical and other social programmes as bait to lure people wholesale into the Christian church, it may be increasingly necessary for Christian missions to give themselves exclusively to the task of planting new churches and seeking to perfect them. As we have already seen, part of the perfecting of the church lies in the impact which it makes upon society as a whole, but *that is the task of the indigenous church rather than that of the international mission.*

The biblical basis for social involvement

1. THE OLD TESTAMENT

In bygone days, confronted with the apparent absence of a social programme in the ministry of the apostles (apart from the early church's provision for its own poor), advocates of 'the social gospel' made a great deal of the scathing denunciations of the Old Testament prophets with their condemnation of social injustice and demand for practical righteousness. It is, however, questionable whether the people of God as a theocracy in possession of the five books of revealed law may be taken as normative when considering the secular nations of today. While the prophets did have messages for other nations their prime task would seem to have been directed towards calling upon the people of Israel to become credible as a community of God, and the application should more properly be made to the church.

We can draw biblical principles of general validity from the Old Testament. In his Singapore Congress Paper, B. E. Fernando of Sri Lanka reminded us that Leviticus and Deuteronomy demonstrate that God is concerned with all the life of all the family. God cares especially for the underprivileged, widows, orphans and immigrants and demands justice in society. We need to be careful, however, in the inferences we draw from the particulars of the Old Testament, which might lead us to affirm, for example, that monarchy is the only divinely sanctioned form of government, that slavery is an acceptable social institution or that adultery and homosexual acts should be punished by the death penalty. David Clines points out some of the problems in interpreting Old Testament precedents in social responsibility.[2] There is:

a. The difference between Israelite and 20th century society It would be difficult to reintroduce the customs of Israelite society (recognizing that this also varies widely throughout its history) into our own period. Young people would be distressed to discover that nobody would lend them enough capital to buy a house. The loan could hardly be repaid in six years, as would be the case with the reintroduction of the Sabbatical year in which all debts were cancelled.

b. The identity of church and state Israel is both a worshipping community, the people of God (church), and also the nation ruled by kings and governed by bureaucrats (state). How are we to distinguish between state law

---

[2] D. A. J. Clines, 'Social Responsibility in the Old Testament'. Paper reproduced in the *Christian Brethren Research Fellowship of New Zealand*, Issue No. 72.

and religious law? How much may we regard as part of Israeli institution and culture and how much as an expression of God's universal will for all men generally?

c. *The Old Testament as the Word of God* Our problems arise precisely because we maintain that the Old Testament is the Word of God in just the same way as the New Testament. David Clines helpfully points out that the Old Testament gives us a series of concrete examples of the outworking of faith in God and the will of God. It shows us the kind of issues to which our faith may be relevant, though the outworking may be completely different in our own time. The Israelite society, with its strong kinship ties, made orphans and strangers particularly under-privileged; so the Old Testament legislates on their behalf. Today other sections of the community may need such support.

Clines' section on *slavery* is quite fascinating, for he suggests that in fact the provisions of the law are essentially destructive to the whole institution of slavery. Slaves are not allowed to work on the Sabbath day (Dt. 5:14: '. . . so that your male and your female servant may rest as well as you'). Slaves are to be released in the Sabbatical year and given a generous severance bonus (Dt. 15:13–14: 'And when you set him free, you shall not send him away empty-handed. You shall furnish him liberally from your flock and from your threshing floor and from your wine vat; you shall give to him as the Lord your God has blessed you'). Moreover, escaped slaves were not to be surrendered to their masters (Dt. 23:15–16: 'You shall not hand over to his master a slave who has escaped from his master to you. He shall live with you in your midst . . .; you shall not mistreat him').

What could be more destructive to the institution of slavery? For if slaves are allowed to remain free once they have escaped then the institution would seem to have little hope of survival. While there is no direct confrontation or explicit prohibition of slavery it is so hedged with conditions that it becomes pointless.

It is indeed remarkable to think that earnest Bible-believing Christians 125 years ago were defending slavery as biblical (even though 1 Tim. 1:10 specifies 'kidnappers' according to the law; Ex. 21:16, Dt. 24:7).[3] Perhaps some who are equally dogmatic on the subjection of women on biblical grounds will also one day have second thoughts.

These brief comments on Old Testament interpretation show that we have no excuse for laziness. We cannot solve these issues by pulling a few proof verses out of context as though they necessarily settled our problems. Scripture must be rigorously compared with Scripture and each one looked at carefully in its own socio-historical context.

2. THE NEW TESTAMENT

a. The Gospels The teaching of Jesus is characterized by deep concern for needy humanity expressed in a practical manner. A very useful article by Howard Marshall provides a valuable summary of the social teaching of Jesus:[4]

i. *Jesus cared for those who were in physical need, notably by healing the sick and feeding the hungry.*

ii. *He sought to restore the outcast to society. In this respect his attitude to Samaritans, publicans, harlots and sufferers from leprosy is noteworthy.*

iii. *He taught that men should care for the poor. The rich young ruler, Zacchaeus and the rich man Dives are sufficient examples.*

iv. *He commended caring for the helpless, condemning putting stumbling blocks in the way of children and, by his attitude*

---

[3] Around 1755 the SPG missionary Thomas Thompson, who had worked first among Negro slaves in New Jersey, and then in the Gold Coast until ill health sent him home, wrote a tract entitled 'The African Trade for Negro Slaves shown to be consistent with the Principles of Humanity and with the Laws of Revealed Religion'. See Geoffrey Moorhouse, *The Missionaries* (Eyre, Methuen, 1973). p.35.

[4] I. H. Marshall, 'The Implications of Christ's Teaching and Ministry', *Christian Graduate*, September 1964.

to divorce, seeking to ensure that women were not cast upon the street without means of livelihood.

v. *He stood out against vested interests. Notably these were the vested interests of religious people, including the bazaars of Annas in the temple courts, the Corban vows, and so on.*

vi. *He gave teaching on political matters, reminding men of their duty to the state.*

As Marshall says, the Christian attitude is not merely humanitarian, for it is characterized by primary reference to the will of God. It is God's *will* that men should love their neighbours and take practical steps to help them.

b. Acts and the epistles There seems little evidence that the New Testament church engaged in a specifically social programme directed towards outsiders, although the following points are worthy of note:

i. *Miracles of healing, although like Christ's own miracles these may be regarded as primarily evidential.*

ii. *The apparently shortlived practice of a common purse in Jerusalem, possibly due to a boycott imposed by the Jews.[5]*

iii. *The later collection for the needy saints in Jerusalem.*

iv. *The serving of tables and the care of widows, although this seems to have been concerned primarily with service to those within the church. The 'helps' (antilēmpseis) of 1 Corinthians 12:28 relates to the cognate verb used by Paul in Acts 20:35: 'You must help the weak'.*

v. *The command to do good to all men, especially those of the household of faith, and the consequent emphasis upon good works (e.g. Tit. 2:7, 14; 3:8, 14 etc.). It does not seem possible to maintain that the church as a new community was concerned to care only for its own poor and its own widows. There was also a concern to be helpful to society as a whole and the 'beautiful' (kalos) deeds of God's people are to be seen by men that they might glorify the*

---

[5] However, it is argued by Max Delespesse in *The Church Community – Leaven and Lifestyle* (Ave Maria Press, Indiana, 1973) that this pooling of goods in Christian communities continued roughly until the Edict of Milan in 312 AD (p.31).

Father in heaven (*Mt. 5:16*). It seems difficult, however, to find much evidence that the New Testament church saw itself as responsible for 'reforming the structures of society'.

vi. The pastoral epistles not only speak of provision being made for the widows[6] but also of enrolling those widows and putting them to work bringing up children, showing hospitality to strangers, washing the saints' feet, assisting those in distress and devoting themselves to every good work (*1 Tim. 5:10*).

The implications of Christian doctrine

This review of biblical teaching has of necessity been brief, but it does seem worth while suggesting some further lines of thought concerning Christian social responsibility.

1. CREATION AND PROVIDENCE

Because of the doctrine of the fall which we see as spoiling God's perfect creation we forget that although creation as a whole was 'very good', as far as man is concerned it was perfect only in the sense in which a baby is perfect. It was envisaged that men would need to be fruitful and multiply and replenish the earth and have dominion over it. As Graham Dow suggests in a recent Shaftesbury Project Paper,[7] we need to think of the creation of man as more like the setting up of a new colony in America by the Pilgrim Fathers; or, to use a more contemporary analogy, the establishment by a group of astronauts of a new colony on some hitherto uninhabited planet. Man receives a mandate from God to have dominion over creation and to develop it for God's glory.

---

[6] 1 Tim. 5:3 where 'honour' would seem to refer to financial support as does the 'double honour' to the elders in 1 Tim. 5:17. It may well be that to honour one's father and mother implies financial support and thus the particular offence of the Corban. See Mk. 7:10–13.

[7] G. Dow, *Dark Satanic Mills?* (Shaftesbury Project, Oxford Street, Nottingham, 1979), p.9.

God is the Creator of *all men* and he continues to care for all men. He makes his sun to rise on the just and the unjust (Mt. 5:45). The point of this passage is that Christian perfection binds us to be equally concerned for God and for the men whom God has made and for whom he cares. This is lucidly worked out by A. N. Triton in his book *Whose World?*[8] An undue emphasis on God as Saviour and a failure to emphasize equally God as Creator and Preserver leads to a distorted Christian doctrine of 'things'; that is, of the material world, the human body and human social structures. He suggests that some of the greatest errors result from a failure to have a proper Christian view of the non-personal factors in human life and experience. He goes on to say that from God's creation and providence, 'all men, indiscriminately may benefit. Food, health, fruitful seasons, science, technology, literature and art, rich family life and excellent stable marriages may be enjoyed by pagans, atheists and heretics.'[9] Thus it would seem a fair assumption that we should care about these things, too, and consequently that we should love men . . . with all that that means.

At the same time Triton speaks out strongly against woolly talk about the 'redemption of society' which 'sounds pious and biblical and is often swallowed without critical examination . . . Redemption is not an infection of social structures, an adjustment of relations, spreading horizontally through society. It results in individuals restored to a right relationship to God. But that sets up horizontal shock waves in society from which all of us benefit. These benefits are in terms of *reforming* society according to God's *law* and not *redeeming* it by the death of Christ.'[10]

[8] A. N. Triton, *Whose World?* (IVP, 1970).
[9] *Ibid.*, p.18.
[10] *Ibid.*, pp.34–35.

2. MAN

Man is created in the image of God and while this image has been marred by the fall it has not been battered out of all recognition. At least two injunctions in the New Testament are based upon this fact (1 Cor. 11:7; Jas. 3:9). Man made in the image of God, even when in sin and rebellion, is of concern to God and should be of concern to us. God's concern is expressed toward man in his present life and most biblical injunctions are about how we are to treat our neighbours in this present world, rather than how we are to treat them in heaven. Interestingly, it is extraordinarily difficult to find direct commands in the New Testament telling churches or Christians to evangelize. There is no lack of command, however, about personal and social responsibilities.

3. THE LAST THINGS

We may well ask why we should struggle for a better world if we know that this world is doomed to destruction. The prospects offered to us in biblical apolcalyptic mean that we are basically pessimistic about the final outcome on earth. We do not anticipate a kingdom of God on earth, not even Jerusalem built 'in England's green and pleasant land'! Our attitude is well expressed in the following quotation:

> The Christian should participate in social and political efforts in order to have an influence in the world, not with the hope of making a paradise, but simply to make it more tolerable. Not to diminish the opposition between this world and the kingdom of God, but simply to modify the opposition between the disorder of this world and the order of preservation that God wants it to have. Not to bring in the kingdom of God, but so that the gospel might be proclaimed, in order that all men might truly hear the Good News.[11]

[11] Jacques Ellul, quoted by Carl Henry in *Aspects of Social Ethics* (Eerdmans, 1964), p.96.

4. CHRISTIAN DISCIPLESHIP

Samuel Escobar makes great use of John Stott's Bible readings at the Berlin Congress, explaining that the words 'As the Father sent me, so send I you' mean that Christ not only gave a command to evangelize, but also provided the model for evangelization.[12] The Word did not merely disguise himself as man, but became flesh and identified with an ill-favoured social class in a country exploited by colonialism. His redemptive task required this identification, this living as a man in the midst of men. As Christ identified himself with men in order to serve them, so should we. Escobar goes on to say that we should follow, not only in the way of incarnation but also in the way of the cross. The one who is sent as Christ was sent is called to travel a similar road of humiliation and sacrifice. We are invited to die for the people we want to serve. There must be a willingness to lose one's life, to fall into the ground and die. Thus Escobar writes:

> Our gospel is false if it leads us to believe that after an encounter with Christ and conversion, the property owner continues to do whatever he feels like doing with his property: the capitalist stops smoking or being an adulterer, but goes on exploiting his workmen: the policeman distributes New Testaments in the prison but continues to torture prisoners in order to secure their confessions: the young rebels are converted into good boys who finished their educational career to get married and tithe so that the church can build a luxurious building with air conditioning, carpeting and velvet curtains.[13]

It becomes clear then that we are wrong if we regard fulfilling our responsibilities to the state, society and to our fellow men as a side-track from evangelism and preaching the gospel. *We must not be so single-eyed in relation*

[12] Samuel Escobar, 'The social impact of the gospel' in Brian Griffiths (ed.), *Is Revolution Change?* (IVP, 1972), pp.89–90.

[13] *Ibid.*, p.141.

to the great commission that we ignore the great commandments.
While we may recognize that missionary societies are
groups of Christians united together to fulfil specific and
limited objectives, this must be set in a total biblical
framework. As missionary societies we do exist primarily
to preach the gospel, to teach disciples, plant churches
and perfect churches. But in order to be effective in doing
those things the preachers must demonstrate the impact
of the gospel of Christ upon their own lives. Those who
teach others to obey all the commandments that Jesus
taught must themselves seek to obey them all and not
merely the last one. Disciples must be taught to love their
neigbours as themselves. The churches which are planted
must not be isolationist ghettos concerned only for their
own salvation and helping their fellow-Christians like
some mutual benefit society. They must be manifestly a
colony of heaven, out-living pagan society around them
and demonstrating by beautiful works the kind of God to
whom they belong. Moreover, the perfecting of the church
will be achieved not merely by its own internal exercises,
but by its members going out together in the face of
opposition to serve the whole community in the name of
Christ. Perfecting the church must mean to develop both
individually and corporately a beautiful lifestyle in relation to the world around. Let me close this section with
a very moving quotation from René Padilla:

> I refuse, therefore, to drive a wedge between a primary task,
> namely the proclamation of the Gospel, and a secondary (at
> best) or even optional (at worst) task of the church. In order
> to be obedient to its Lord the church should never do anything
> that is not essential; therefore, nothing that the church does
> in obedience to its Lord is unessential. Why? Because love to
> God is inseparable from love to men; because faith without
> works is dead; because hope includes the restoration of all
> things to the Kingdom of God. I am not confusing the two
> kingdoms – I do not expect the ultimate salvation of man or
> society through good works or political action. I am merely

asking that we take seriously the relevance of the Gospel to the totality of man's life in the world.[14]

The history of missions and social involvement

It is commonly believed that missionaries in the countries dominated by Western colonial powers and commercial interests failed to speak out against the economic and political oppression which hindered the development of the nationals. Doubtless some evidence could be found to support this, but there is much evidence on the other side which is often disregarded. *David Livingstone* first wakened the Christian conscience to the guilt of the white man on the west coast and of the Arab on the east coast who were carrying Africans into slavery.[15]

It is less well known that Christians were involved in constant protest and lobbying against the evils of the *opium trade*. A Japanese Christian student once asked me whether Hudson Taylor had ever said anything in protest concerning the opium traffic, and I was unable at that time to reply. Reference to bound copies of *China's Millions* (CIM's magazine) makes it abundantly clear that the China Inland Mission did a great deal to acquaint the Christian public with what was happening. In the bound edition of 1878, for example, the preface mentions the opium traffic on the very first page and comments that 'the Christian missionary has no greater hindrance to his usefulness than the prejudice excited against him on account of our country's connection with the opium trade.' It goes on to say that because of people's ignorance of the traffic and England's responsibility for it they have felt it a solemn duty to give the information 'in the hope that they may be led to earnest and prayerful action for

[14] René Padilla, 'Evangelism and the World', *LTEHHV*, pp.144–145.
[15] Stephen Neill, *History of Christian Missions* (Penguin, 1964), p.316.

the delivery of our beloved country from continued complicity in this iniquitous business'.[16]

The same issue also contains accounts of famine in China accompanied by lurid drawings of what famine means, showing cannibalism, suicide and death by starvation. The CIM did not hesitate to point out that the total amount given that year for famine relief in China (some £40,000) was equivalent to the profit gained by Britain from opium in two days. This same volume includes no less than twenty-five references in the course of the year (and covering several pages) on the subject of *famine relief.* And in an edition as late as 1901, under the heading 'The Greatest Crime of the Century' there is a diagram of a clock indicating that an average of half a ton of opium had been exported to China during every hour of Victoria's sixty glorious years (1837–1897). 'Would that British Christians would unceasingly labour and pray that England's connection with this terrible trade may be speedily ended. Our guilt in this matter is appalling.' (It should be noticed, however, that this strong social protest was directed by missionaries to their own government and not to the government of China in which country they were guests.)

There is an anecdote told of asking a missionary to Korea, 'What are you doing in the way of social reform?', to which the missionary replied, 'Nothing. We are too busy preaching the gospel.' The fact remains that the gospel has made greater progress in Korea than in any other country in Asia! Does this suggest that too much emphasis upon social programmes is a side-track? Certainly the Nevius plan for foreign missions delivered the

[16] In the index, under the letter 'O', there are no less than *ten entries in this one year on the subject of opium traffic* including a series of eight letters by F. S. Mander (accompanied by black and white drawings of opium smoking and suffering caused by it), an article by no less a personage than His Excellency, the Prime Minister of the Chinese Empire, and also a letter from the Chinese ambassador, Kuo Sung-tao, from Langham Place, London.

Korean Church from Western paternalism and from being dependent upon foreign money for the erection of church buildings and for the support of its pastors. The absence of foreign money also meant that there were no extensive social programmes. It is noticeable, too, that the greatest spiritual progress seems to have been made in a country where there has been a good deal of material poverty.

On a visit to the museum in Johannesburg I was somewhat surprised to discover hostile comment about some of the early missionaries to South Africa. One for example was described as a 'noted negrophilist' (*i.e.*, a lover of black people). I wondered what lay behind this hostile attitude towards some of the early missionaries by Bible-loving Afrikaaners who, it will be remembered, migrated northward in the Great Trek to escape the growing British dominance in the Cape. It seems that the missionaries got much closer to the indigenous people and, finding them enslaved by the Boer farmers, supported the black African against exploitation, insisting that slavery was now abolished within the British empire. It was interesting to find this testimony, from a hostile source, of the developed social conscience of some early missionaries.

It is plain that when missionaries were related directly to a colonial power some did seek to exert a Christian influence and did not ignore social and political events.

The special problems of Christian *diakonia* (service)

1. *DIAKONIA* AND PROSELYTIZATION

Unsympathetic governments may allege (and in India this has been a frequent charge) that the only reason why people convert to Christianity is that the missionaries are offering them material inducements to do so. However much Christians reply that their concern is only for genuine converts, the charge will still be made. It was made as early as September 1880 in Tientsin, when Viceroy Li

Hung-Chang remarked to Timothy Richard: '. . . should mercenary advantages be withdrawn from the so-called Christian converts of the poor and ignorant lower classes, there would soon be no more Christians in China, for certainly Christianity has made no inroads among the educated and thinking classes.'[17] These were the celebrated 'rice Christians' who saw their membership of the foreign-financed church pragmatically: a useful insurance and hedge against famine.

Present-day feeling in the Islamic world is very strong, as evidenced recently at a dialogue held in June 1976: a five-day consultation on Christian mission and Islamic *da'wah*. For example, Professor Khurshid Ahmad, Director General of the Islamic Foundation in Leicester, commented as follows:

> The methodology of Christian mission concentrated upon influencing the object in a state of weakness and helplessness. Instead of direct invitation, approaches were made to those who were disadvantaged, exploiting their weaknesses for the sake of proselytism. The poor, the sick and the immature were made special targets of economic assistance, medical aid and education. Many a Christian mission acted as an organic part of colonialism and cultural imperialism. All this was a very unfair way to bring people to any religion.[18]

The conference finally produced a statement urging that both Christian and Islamic minorities should be entitled to live their religious lives in accordance with their religion in perfect freedom and stating that the attitudes expressed were reciprocal, recognizing fully the rights of Christians in Muslim countries, as well as Muslims in Christian countries. It went on to say, however, that 'The Conference strongly condemns all such abuse of *diakonia* (service). Its Christian members disassociate themselves in the name of Christianity from any service which has

[17] Spencer J. Palmer, *Korea and Christianity* (Holym, 1967), p.25.
[18] *IRM*, October 1976, p.368

degraded itself by having any purpose whatever beside *agapē* (love for God and neighbour). They declare that any *diakonia* undertaken for any ulterior motive is a propaganda instrument and not an expression of *agapē*.[19] The conference went on to urge Christian churches and religious organizations to 'suspend their misused *diakonia* in Muslim countries'. It was recommended that all material aid be distributed through governments and the local people to whom the aid was given. In this way the aggravated relations might be eased.

It can be seen that the drift of this most recent discussion is a very strong incentive for the abandonment of the practice of missions of sending out doctors, nurses, agricultural and economic experts, in favour of concentrating on straightforward presentation of the Christian gospel — to be considered on its merits and not unfairly buttressed by being included in a package with various other material goodies which are the largesse of wealthier developed countries. The ironic thing is that so often visas have been refused to missionaries whose prime intention has been straightforward preaching of the gospel and the planting and perfecting of churches, and granted only for people who have had some other reason for entry, *e.g.*, medical, agricultural or academic. The conference went on to recognize that mission and *da'wah* are essential religious duties of both Christianity and Islam, and that the purpose of suspending misused *diakonia* is to re-establish mission in the future on a religiously sound basis, acceptable to both. But it is highly questionable whether countries which are predominantly Muslim will permit Christian missionaries, shorn of all foreign aid and medical and agricultural skills, to enter and to engage in direct dialogue evangelism among Muslims. Most recent evidence is of deliberate anti-Christian discrimination.

[19] *Ibid.*, p.458.

2. HOSTILITY TO SOCIAL PROGRAMS

It is sometimes blithely imagined that the involvement and engagement of Christian missionaries in social programmes is going to be received with howls of delight and enthusiastic approval all round. This is not necessarily the case. Those who are more fortunate or more privileged may not appreciate the concern of the foreigner for depressed and under-privileged minorities. Let me give just three recent examples.

In the Philippines missionaries discovered that the lowland Filipino was constantly exploiting the tribal peoples living in the mountains. These people would clear the ground for agriculture only suddenly to be evicted by a lowlander who had taken pains to lay a claim on the land and thus to make it legally his. To begin with the tribal people did not understand that the land was not automatically theirs and that other people could just take it from them. At a later stage attempts were made by tribal people to get the land registered as theirs and unscrupulous officials would take their money but 'forget' to register it properly. Missionaries stuck their necks out in protesting against this injustice and on a number of occasions got into serious trouble for doing so. Very wonderfully, in due course, the Philippine Lawyers Christian Fellowship was formed and Christian lowlanders provided legal aid, either totally free or for a token payment, to enable the aboriginal people to lay title to the land on which they had lived and laboured for generations. This example is a very thrilling one in that Christian nationals took over from the missionaries the responsibility of social justice. It should be noted, however, that the missionary who supports a minority group is not necessarily popular.

Another example was in North Thailand where missionaries were seeking to help the Akha tribe, one of the poorest and most backward of the tribal minority groups. Work parties of young Swiss came out to help in their summer holidays and various agricultural implements were supplied to help the Akha transfer from the 'slash and burn' nomadic culture to a more scientific agriculture. This was not necessarily appreciated by their Northern Thai neighbours. The hut containing the agricultural implements was broken into and all the handles sawn off to render them useless; houses in the tribal village were deliberately set on fire. For a while it was even suspected that the murder of one of the Swiss missionaries was due to such hostility, brought about by foreigners who were spending time and money on nomadic people and in the process of building a teacher's house in their village. We may understand the situation better by imagining the setting up of a caravan encampment in the neighbourhood of an English village. If some well-meaning Christian came along and established a permanent school or church building or an evangelist's house in the middle of such an encampment, one can envisage the hostility this would generate among villagers hopeful that the 'minority group' would soon be moving on!

In Central Thailand a scheme was launched to help leprosy patients to become financially self-supporting by supplying them with piglets, ducklings and chicks. But unscrupulous neighbours were ready to steal or kill off this livestock, resenting the betterment of their poor neighbours.

These difficulties are no reason for not engaging in such work. But it needs to be recognized that Christian good works will not necessarily bring local approval.

3. TECHNOLOGY AND MATERIALISM

When the Mission to Lepers was originally founded there was no known cure for leprosy and the mission existed to bring 'the consolation of the gospel' to those who suffered from this horrible disease. Today, renamed the Leprosy Mission, this society can work to halt the progress of the disease, perform tendon transplant operations and restore the function of hands and feet. Physiotherapists and occupational therapists can rehabilitate patients so that they can earn their own living and regain their self-respect. It should be added that the preaching of the resurrection of the body 'refashioned like unto his glorious body' is a teaching that brings even greater encouragement than do these more immediate practical benefits. At the funeral of the kidnapped and murdered OMF leprosy nurses, Margaret Morgan and Minka Hanskamp, in South Thailand, a former Muslim leprosy patient testified to the love these two Christian women expressed as they took his ulcerated and leprous feet upon their knees, bathed and treated them and bound them up.

At the same time it must be recognized that the techniques which are used by the Leprosy Mission in particular and Christian hospitals in general are in no sense a consequence of Christianity, but a product of modern Western science and technology. Certainly the missionary doctor is moved by Christian compassion but what he uses are the products of Western science. The effectiveness of scientific remedies has nothing directly to do with belief in Christ. Social contributions will certainly show the advantages of the scientific and technological society, but this is as likely to introduce materialism as to introduce the Christian gospel. We may rescue people from the frying pan of primitive superstition only to drop them into the fire of worldly materialism.

One immediately questions how right it is for Western missionaries to use their 'superior technology and scientific knowledge' to lure the tribal person into becoming a Christian. Medicine, education, financial aid, agricultural implements and techniques are regarded by unsympathetic people as *bait to gain followers*. It is the old problem of 'rice Christians' in a new guise: winning men who have materialistic motives. In obedience to Christ's command we must demonstrate Christian care and compassion *for their own sake*.

4. DEPENDENCE UPON THE FOREIGNER

There is a further problem in that material aid produces dependence upon the foreigner. Whilst such service may be carried out from the highest motives, this kind of paternalism does not produce strong independent Christian communities, but rather a dependent parasitic group ingratiating itself with the foreigner for the sake of various side benefits.

The pioneer missionary Robert Moffat arrived in South Africa with the London Missionary Society in 1817, when he was 21 years of age. He wrote in his journal: 'We preach, we converse, we catechize, but without the least apparent success. Only satiate their mendicant spirits by perpetually giving, and you are all that is good; but refuse to meet their endless demands and their theme of praise is turned to ridicule and abuse. . . .'[20]

When I was visiting Wycliffe Hall for the Chavasse lectures, a student who had served in the American Armed Forces remarked how totally nauseating was the attitude of many national people towards the American GI. There were always those who were ready to flatter and butter up and ingratiate themselves with the apparently wealthy foreigner in order to get him to pay for things. Every American base had this surrounding area of parasitic industries. On nothing like the same scale, but none the less present, is the tendency of some to want to identify with the missionary's apparent wealth, health and prosperity and to fail to distinguish between what is distinctively Christian and what are only the products of Western civilization.

This is, of course, a long-standing problem. And it is an important factor to bear in mind in the remarkable response to the Christian gospel in a country like Korea. While manifestly the work of the Holy Spirit is involved, it cannot be overlooked that the existing belief in a

[20] Geoffrey Moorhouse, *The Missionaries*, p.65.

supreme being and the identification of Christianity with opposition to Japanese Shinto imperialism were very significant factors, as was identification with 'Christian' America in preference to its three powerful threatening neighbours, Russia, China and Japan. That such factors may be influential and used by the Holy Spirit we cannot deny, but whether as Christians we should as deliberate strategy ally ourselves with political and material trends is an entirely different matter.

5. BEING A GUEST

The missionary faces particular problems above and beyond those of a Christian residing as a citizen in his own land. Most missionaries today are aliens and guests permitted to reside in other countries on a visitor's visa. The missionary's comments on political and economic issues are not particularly welcome and may result in the withdrawal of his visa and possible repercussions for others associated with him. It was one thing for Hudson Taylor and his colleagues to protest vigorously against British complicity in opium traffic and even to mar their own Queen's Jubilee celebrations by pointing out that in every hour of those sixty allegedly glorious years an average of half a ton of opium had left India for China. They could draw attention to these inconsistencies because they were British citizens. But the missionary who sees it as his vocation to point out the shortcomings of governments in whose countries he is a visitor is likely to make a speedy departure. There is an entertaining illustration of this in Professor Enright's *Memoirs of a Mendicant Professor* when, in his inaugural lecture as Professor of English at Singapore University, he was unwise enough to make some amusing comments about Malay culture. He was publicly rebuked in the press and told that he was paid to teach English and that when political advice was required he would be asked for it!

The guest then is torn between civility and integrity. And we cannot so easily shrug off our responsibilities.

Missionaries normally keep quiet, concentrating on a pietistic type of salvation, quietening their conscience by saying 'We are guests here, we have no business to criticize. But when we behave like this we are *not* neutral, we are simply supporting the *status quo*. That is often a terrible thing to do, for Christianity is *not* the same as middle-class conservatism. Oh for a return of the spirit of prophecy to our ministries. Amos was told to go home to Judah or shut up. But he did not use the 'guest' excuse.[21]

So, when does a guest speak out? Even if it means being thrown out? And will anybody listen?

6. A LIMITED BUDGET

Christian financial resources are limited and often the social needs are extremely great. When conditions of economic distress and famine cannot be solved by the government of India or even by all the resources of the United Nations together with philanthropic organizations like Oxfam, Save the Children and so on, it seems almost farcical for missionary societies to enter into this field at all. If we cannot change the circumstances of life (which legally constituted governments and the United Nations cannot change either) it might be better to concentrate on offering the Christian faith which will both

a. help people to triumph over those temporal circumstances and

b. motivate people to improve the societies in which they live.

As B. E. Fernando points out in various of his writings, many of India's problems could be dealt with by the introduction of family planning and by dealing with graft and corruption. When large stores of food go every year to feed large numbers of sacred cattle which may not even be eaten by human beings, it may be added that the first

---

[21] Dick Dowsett, 'How we must be prepared to answer the Marxist approach to social issues', a paper given at Philippines Missionary Conference, 1971.

requirement in dealing with famine is to overcome the negative effects of Hindu superstition. Christian giving for famine relief may be serving only to stave off the collapse of Hinduism! Thus, while it is all very well for the Wheaton Congress to declare that 'evangelicals are increasingly convinced that they must involve themselves in the great social problems men are facing', the difficult question remains: how far should we directly involve ourselves in 'great social problems'?

7. THE NECESSITY OF LIMITED GOALS

Missionary societies usually have specific and limited aims in terms of church planting and church perfecting. Their direct involvement in 'great social problems' must therefore be limited. This statement, however, needs qualifying in two ways. First, the Christian church must always give a balanced presentation of what obedience to Christ means. It must not only believe theoretically but demonstrate practically its obedience to the great commission and to the great commandments. Thus the pioneer missionary must both preach and look for opportunity to show the reality of his faith by his works.

It is easy to imagine pioneer missionaries in the mountains as muscular Christians whose aim is 'not to reason why'. But they also need thoughtful sensitivity.

Tribal societies do not departmentalize the activities of life into tightly sealed-off compartments. Life is a unity. All the parts are inter-related and integrated into a comprehensive whole. It is not possible for missionaries to approach the religious without involving the physical . . . especially in a tribal context. The whole manner of the missionary's life witnesses as much as his preaching. The national carefully observes how he lives, what he is, his reactions, his basic attitudes. . . . Even though our sole intention is to preach the gospel, we cannot help working in a comprehensive manner. We see sickness treated by animistic remedies. Moved by compassion we introduce Western drugs. We see poverty largely due to extremely primitive agricultural methods and tribal superstitions, so we introduce seeds, chemical fertilizers and Western technology. Gradually we become more and more enmeshed in service as well as preaching, often hoping that such assistance will open tribal hearts to the preaching of the gospel.[22]

The pioneer missionary has to do this because he is all the church there is. But he needs to be aware of the very real problems and act wisely in order to forestall them.

At a later stage, where the church already exists, the missionary may find himself much more free to concentrate upon preaching and teaching, provided he has taught the young church that good works are essential, that the total witness of the Christian community must involve both the horizontal as well as the vertical dimension. Thus while missionary societies may deliberately refrain from unnecessary involvement in socio-economic matters, they can recognize how *vital* is such involvement for the emerging churches. Education, social and economic services are possible only if a Christian congregation has grown up on the mission field.

Thus the primary work of the Christian minister is not to be a social worker but a teacher of the Word of God. *But* both the national minister and the foreign missionary must also indicate the relevance of the teaching of Scripture to the socio-economic situation. While the missionary or minister may not himself be called to direct involvement in socio-political matters, the members of his congregation *are*, if they are to exercise their God-given function as salt and light. The preacher/teacher may be thought of as the driving wheel of the congregation motivated by the force and power of God's Word. He must ensure that his teeth engage with the multiple cogs of the several church members. If the church is to be effective

[22] James Morris, 'The Relationship of Social Work to the Gospel', a paper given at an OMF North Thailand missionaries' conference.

as a witness to the glory of God in society as a whole, and effective in evangelism, the teeth of these lay members in turn must bite into that society, must be 'engaged' in order that the motive force of the Word, transmitted through the teacher to the congregation, may begin to 'turn the world upside down'. It may be true that the pioneer missionary is 'too busy preaching the gospel' but if he is to declare the whole counsel of God, he dare not be too busy to teach the social law of God.

Here are some useful warnings from a Third World writer, B. E. Fernando, reminding us to keep our goals clear:

> If we concentrate our efforts on trying to improve man's environment alone, even if we succeed, we are only bringing him back to the Garden of Eden and the story of the fall would be repeated. Are we not trying to convince ourselves nowadays that if we gain the whole world it matters not what happens to our soul, but if we seek first the 'other things' the kingdom of God will be added. Heaven is not hell air-conditioned. . . . There seem to be as many problems in the developed countries as in the developing countries – only they are different in nature though equally damaging in effect. There is a grave danger in allowing the world to provide the agenda of the church. Said Dean Inge a generation ago: 'If you marry the spirit of your own generation you will be a widow in the next.'[23]

8. ALTRUISM AND INTENT

We want to serve the whole man, body and soul, not only meeting man's material needs but urging him to be reconciled to God through Christ. But then we begin to be troubled. Are we being sufficiently altruistic? Or are

[23] B. E. Fernando, 'Integral Development – Reflections of a Conservative Evangelical from a Developing Country', *IRM*, October 1969, pp.409, 401.

we in danger of using our medical or social work as bait to bring people to Christ?

If we are engaged in straight planting of new congregations in a pioneer area we have no such worries. If we are working at church perfecting at the invitation of a national church, again we have no problems. But if we find ourselves involved in a predominantly social ministry we are constantly being troubled by our own motivation, and this sometimes causes us to be silent. We fail to speak for Christ and to minister to man's spiritual needs when we ought to be doing so.

Many Christian workers in Bangladesh have been allowed to enter as medical missionaries or as suppliers of social services only on the understanding that they will not proselytize. Sometimes they are even asked to sign statements that they will not do so. For a Christian not to preach Christ is a denial of the essence of the Christian gospel. It is a basic tenet of Christianity, in obedience to the commands of Christ, that we seek to make disciples of all nations. Missionaries in such circumstances often find themselves tied up in knots as they seek to determine what is and what is not ethically possible for them.

9. DEVELOPMENT AND THE END OF *DIAKONIA*

In many Western countries voluntary Christian societies which gave themselves to good works have ultimately been replaced by the state providing its own welfare services. In the same kind of way it is surely evident that it is the goal of every responsible government in a developing country to provide its own schools, hospitals and leprosy services and to train its own national doctors, nurses and agriculturalists. Any theory of mission, then, which leans too heavily on these 'supplementary ministries' is bound to find that its sphere of ministry is increasingly curtailed. This needs seriously to be borne in mind when speaking today of missionary recruitment. The overwhelming need is still for evangelists and church planters and for those who will work in a humble role at the invitation of national churches. In unevangelized countries 'old-fashioned missionaries' will still be needed when medical and agricultural specialists are no longer required. This is the chief fallacy of the ecumenical approach to mission.

Conclusions

Social action illustrates and prepares the way for the preaching of the cross, but it is also *justified for its own sake* and not merely as a lever for evangelism. We do not practise medicine just as a means of saving souls, but because it is right and according to the will of God to help our fellow men to health. Evangelical motivation for social action has sometimes been too shallow. John Stott comments helpfully on evangelism and social action when he writes:

> The two are partners in the Christian mission; indeed, to use Ron Sider's expression, 'distinct yet equal' partners. Neither is an excuse for the other, a cloak for the other or a means to the other. Each exists in its own right as an expression of Christian love. Both should be included in some degree in every local church's programme.[24]

Missionary societies must engage in philanthropy as far as they can but leave political action to the nationals. In pioneer missionary work, when the missionary is all the local church there is, some involvement in good works would seem to be essential if the gospel is not to be misunderstood. At a later stage some individual national Christians will be called to concentrate upon direct evangelism, others to a teaching ministry and others to social service. What is important is that the *total ministry* of each local expression of the body of Christ should reflect a biblical balance, like the Salvation Army slogan 'Soup, Soap and Salvation'.

[24] J. R. W. Stott responding to Ronald J. Sider in *Evangelism, Salvation and Social Justice* (Grove Books, 1977), p.22.

Christian motivation for meeting the need of a neighbour is often identified with the parable of the Good Samaritan. On 14 January 1978 a missionary van with seventeen people on board was in collision with a lorry on a road in Thailand. In the wreckage were twelve who were dead and a further five survivors in varying degrees of injury and shock. Here then was the needy neighbour, bleeding to death by the roadside. All of the people concerned were either themselves missionary surgeons and doctors or members of their families: they had come out to serve the whole man and to minister to men's bodies as well as souls. As they lay there in the wreckage by the wayside Thai people came running. Not to help, but to rob and steal and go through the pockets of the dead and unconscious passengers. What greater demonstration could there be that it is not enough to meet men's physical needs alone. Clearly those Thai Buddhists need a change of heart and mind that only Christ can bring about.

It is thus not a question of either/or but rather of both/ and. We must not see the fulfilling of social responsibility as an alternative to our spiritual responsibility to men's souls but as an accompanying demonstration of Christian love and as an enacted parable of the meeting of spiritual need.

Material for study

Samuel Escobar, 'Evangelism and Man's Search for Freedom, Justice and Fulfilment', *LTEHHV*, p.303.
René Padilla, 'Evangelism and the World', *LTEHHV*, p.116.
B. E. Fernando, 'Integral Development', *IRM*, October 1969.
Ronald J. Sider and John R. W. Stott, *Evangelism, Salvation and Social Justice* (Grove Books, 1977).

Questions for discussion

1. What evidence can we find that the apostles were concerned about the material needs of non-Christians?
2. How far is it wise or possible for the missionary who is a

guest in another country to take part in social or political protest against injustice?

3. How can we seek to meet men's material needs without using the products of technology as an inducement to conversion to Christianity? Is it wise for the same people both to serve and preach? Or is it right to divorce preaching from serving?

4. Biblically, how can we reconcile the horizontal and vertical axes of Christian responsibility to God and human society?

5. Is it more biblical to seek to care for the world than to build the church?

4 The confusion of the church and the world

... The mystery of Christ, which in other generations was not made known to the sons of men ... has now been revealed to His holy apostles and prophets in the Spirit; to be specific, *that the Gentiles are fellow-heirs and fellow-members of the body, and fellow-partakers of the promise in Christ Jesus through the gospel. ... To me, the very least of all saints, this grace was given, to preach to the Gentiles the unfathomable riches of Christ, and to bring to light what is the administration of the mystery which for ages has been hidden in God, who created all things; in order that the manifold wisdom of God might now be made known through the church to the rulers and the authorities in the heavenly places. This was in accordance with the eternal purpose which He carried out in Christ Jesus our Lord.* Ephesians 3:4–11

Many of us as simple Christians have understood from passages like this that the church of Jesus Christ is *the* new humanity and *the* new community. We have understood the Bible to say that if men are to be saved they must repent and believe and call upon the name of the Lord and thus be incorporated into his body, the church. Only in Christ and in his body is there salvation. Is this, however, a simplistic misunderstanding of the gospel and of the church? Today, some are arguing that the church only exists for the world, that Christ is the 'man for others' and the church must be the 'church for others'. Thus one of the objections to church growth thinking is that the church should be thinking about others in the world around and not about itself. Once the church becomes preoccupied with itself we are in the realm of ecclesiolatry, not ecclesiology.[1] The church is seen to be ineffective and to have become little more than a pietistic ghetto. As Julian Charley has said, it is as if the church is 'fiddling while Rome burns, so petty are its internal concerns over against the major crises facing humanity . . . *mission has become obsessively church-centred.* The institutionalized church is seen as an end in itself.'[2] He goes on to point out that while we certainly want to repudiate this pettiness and to reject denominationalism, 'the church for the church's sake', it is an entirely different matter to accept the man-focused view that 'the church is held to exist *for the world*'.

In his 1970 William Carey Lectures Dr M. M. Thomas has criticized the historic Christian position as one which relegates the whole of human history, apart from the work of preaching the gospel and expanding the church, to being either lost or, at best, irrelevant. He comments that 'this approach has contributed to the Christian indifference to secular politics which led to the rise of Hitler and Stalin in the West'.[3] Many modern theologians in the West, however, have begun to 'discern Christ's work in human history'. More traditional theologians have recognized this as 'a radical shift of the centre from God to man and accordingly the replacement of theology by anthropology'.

It must be appreciated, as is usually the case in such matters, that a measure of important truth is being expressed here. 'Secular' and 'church' history cannot be separated because God is the Lord of all his creation, whether his sovereignty is recognized or not. And he cares about its fate. 'Humanization is concerned, therefore, with

---

[1] *Cf.* J. G. Davies, 'Church Growth: A Critique', *IRM*, July 1968.

[2] Julian Charley, *Mission – Some Contemporary Trends* (Falcon, 1973), p.10.

[3] M. M. Thomas, 'Salvation and Humanization', *IRM*, January 1971, p.29.

recognizing the hand of God in all areas of world history, even where it is not remotely connected with the church.[4] Just as Jesus became really incarnate in order to identify himself with humanity, so the church must recognize that it is also a part of humanity. This point was repeatedly made at the Uppsala assembly of the World Council of Churches in 1968.

> The world – not only the church, but the world – is God's. Isn't that finally why we abjure all neat bifurcations of church and world: not only because the church is in the world, or the world is in the church, but ultimately operative in both of them is the same God.[5]

This truth, however, needs to be thought through carefully in relation to other biblical doctrine to avoid the kind of confusion in which Mao Tse-Tung's liberation movement, for instance, is seen to fall 'within what Christians understand as God's saving work in history', where the 'Long March' is compared with the exodus and Chairman Mao regarded as a 'saviour'.

> In the case of New China it is still valid to ask whether she is destined to play for future world history the role which ancient Israel has played for the past millennia. . . . Salvation history is present already in the histories of nations, and in this case, in the history of New China. This completely nullifies the old concept of Christian mission as the extension of Western Christendom. Furthermore, it puts into question the validity of mission interest currently shown by certain groups of Western Christians. China might have been lost to the Western churches, but not to God. To advocate the carrying of the banner of the gospel back to China from the West is to deny the presence of God in China through his own acts.[6]

[4] Charley, pp.17–18.

[5] A Lutheran observer quoted in Kenneth Slack, *Uppsala Report* (SCM Press, 1968), p.45.

[6] Choan-Seng Song, 'New China and Salvation History – A Methodological Enquiry' LWF–PIV seminar in Bastad, 1974: 'Theological Implications of the New China'.

We certainly know that God is at work in his church in China and that in spite of persecution from the secular state it has continued to survive and even in some places to grow. At the same time, can we identify that church-persecuting secular state with the 'kingdom of God'? This is just one outstanding example of the remarkable confusion between the church and the world which exists in ecumenical circles today.

The danger of theological selectivity

As with many other theological errors, this problem arises not from entirely mis-stating the truth, but from ignoring and failing to state other complementary truths. As Bruce Nicholls points out, ecumenical theology tends to concentrate upon the axis 'creation – incarnation – resurrection' (*i.e.* ultimate restoration of all things); the facts that God created man, Jesus became a man and the salvation of God is a destiny for man. All of this is gloriously true and to be accepted with thanksgiving.

But there is another biblical axis which is being ignored: that of 'fall – atonement – judgment'. The present tendency is to stress the first axis and to disregard the second. We need to remind our WCC friends that our theology must also make room for the biblical facts that man is fallen and sinful; that salvation is achieved not merely by Jesus becoming man, but by Jesus dying for man on the cross; that he was not bringing God down to man's level but lifting man up to God's level. There is also the serious failure to remember that the purpose of God not only includes the salvation of believing and justified men, but also the judgment of unbelieving and wicked men. The tendency within the World Council of Churches to move from theology to anthropology means not that they are failing to say many true things, but that they are neglecting to place equal emphasis upon the whole counsel of God.

112

The varied nature of God's involvement in history

The Old Testament shows God choosing a particular individual, Abraham, and his descendants. The very idea of 'salvation history' implies specific agents in God's redemptive plan. God did indeed use the Assyrian, Babylonian and Persian kings in the disciplining of his people, but they nevertheless acted from their own selfish motives. Similarly, it would be simplistic today to regard all movements for human rights as evidence of the kingdom of God in action, as some of these 'criticizing' influences spring from selfish motives. To call all this the 'mission of God' obscures the fact that God has a specific task for the church in the history of the world, namely to proclaim Jesus Christ as Lord. This distinction is recognized by Choan-Seng Song:

> Does this mean all theological judgment is about to be suspended and that all historical events will be identified with the acts of God for men's salvation? Not at all. To say that all historical events are God's acts is as meaningless as to say history as such is God's revelation. . . .[7]

The spiritual forces of wickedness which oppose the gospel

It is a common assumption that progress is inevitable, an evolutionary optimism that talks as though the only enemy is ignorance, that once everyone is educated in good liberal opinions all difficulties will disappear. It is an optimism that is plainly naïve.

It ignores first, the evil in the heart of the individual man. Loving your neighbour is the golden rule for every 'other' man, because it is only 'natural' to be selfish and put yourself first. The cartoon of the man apologizing for the magnificent rhinoceros head on his wall reads: 'Had to bag one, Harry, in case this damned conservation thing

[7] Choan-Seng Song, 'New China and Salvation History', p.7.

doesn't work and they become extinct.' It also ignores the evil structures of society that discriminate against people of coloured minorities, that confine wealth to certain classes, that make a few countries rich and keep many more poor. And lastly it ignores the prince of this world and the spiritual forces of wickedness. The purposes of God are actively opposed by satanic forces. Belief in the devil and the powers of evil has been played down as an outworn myth. Writers of fiction, poetry and drama grapple more honestly and passionately with problems of sin and evil than many of our theologians have been doing.

Is there any room in ecumenical theology for belief in the enemy? Liberal theology does not leave much room for the supernatural in any form and even God must be demythologized. There is still less room for the devil and the spiritual forces of wickedness. They may have been part of the biblical world view – that can scarcely be denied – but modern man has tended to identify wickedness solely with human institutions. There seems little readiness to recognize that behind all these lies the devil with all his subtle wiles and snares. Such reductionist theologies dislike separating the sheep from the goats (even over social issues!), and find it impossible to believe in theological wolves (so well disguised in sheep's clothing) even if Christ warned us of such dangers.

Naïve neo-marxist triumphalism

It is really a little naïve to identify Mao's China as the outworking of 'the rule of God' on earth. Bishop Stephen Neill in his Chavasse Lectures[8] neatly brings this into proportion by comparing social justice and other very real advances made in Mao's China with the way in which a century ago Christians of equal intelligence and sincerity interpreted the advance of the colonial powers as a saving act of God. He shows how the establishing of universal peace, the provision of education and medical aid, the

[8] S. Neill, *Salvation Tomorrow* (Lutterworth, 1976), p.73.

improvement in the position of women, emancipation of depressed classes, the abolishing of *sati* and *thuggee* and the development of the famine code all had a tremendous effect in improving the quality of life throughout British India. Yet there are not too many people left today who would wish to equate the British empire with the kingdom of God. One cannot avoid gaining the impression that people who see the primary task of 'salvation' as overthrowing the structures of society are influenced more by marxist thinking (not always unconsciously) than by biblical theology.

Universalism

The underlying theology behind this confusion of the church and the world is the false teaching that ultimately the church and the world will be co-terminous and that nobody will be left outside the church. This doctrine is defined by C. H. Dodd as the belief that, 'as every human being lives under God's judgment, so every human being is ultimately destined in God's mercy to eternal life.'[9] Universalism is also defined in the *Oxford Dictionary of the Christian Church* under the heading:

> Apokatastasis. The Greek name for the doctrine that ultimately all free moral creatures – angels, men and devils – will share in the grace of salvation. It is to be found in Clement of Alexandria, in Origen and in St. Gregory of Nyssa. It was strongly attacked by St. Augustine of Hippo and formally condemned in the first anathema against Origenism, probably put out by the Council of Constantinople in AD 543. . . .[10]

Formal condemnation by the Catholic Church and difficulty in harmonizing it honestly with the teaching of Jesus have possibly prevented this view from being made more explicit.

[9] Quoted by J. I. Packer in 'The Way of Salvation, Part III; The Problems of Universalism', *Bibliotheca Sacra*, 130, January 1973, pp.3–11.
[10] F. L. Cross (ed.), *The Oxford Dictionary of the Christian Church* (OUP, 1958), p.57.

More recently, Archbishop William Temple abandoned any and all ideas of hell.

Such concepts could not permanently remain in the minds of people who read the Gospels. Steadily the conviction has gained ground that the God and Father of our Lord Jesus Christ cannot be conceived as inflicting on any soul that He has made unending torment. . . . How can there be a paradise for any while there is a hell for some? Each supposedly damned soul was born into the world as a mother's child; and paradise there cannot be for her if her child is in such a hell.[11]

Jim Packer writing on this subject says that 'whereas till recently its status was that of a discredited speculation, nowadays it is widely regarded as belonging to orthodoxy. Missionary leaders and major theologians, both Catholic and Protestant, assert more or less explicitly that all will be saved, or at least that the question of their salvation should be left open with the scales of expectation tilted in the universalist direction. . . .'[12]

And in a footnote he adds that 'The names of William Temple, C. H. Dodd, C. Raven, H. H.Farmer, John Hick, John Baillie, N. Berdyaev, C. F. D. Moule, Karl Barth, W. Michaelis, Hans Küng, may be cited as samples to illustrate the assertion in the text.'

Missionary advocates of universalism

This 'Trojan Horse' has gained entrance into Christendom and threatens to destroy missionary motives and hinder the effectiveness of Christ's soldiers and their readiness to continue the battle . . . perhaps there is no battle! The church militant is to be militant no longer! The effect of this doctrine upon missions can be seen from the following quotation:

The question of authority is immediately linked with the

[11] W. Temple, 'The Idea of Immortality in Relation to Religion and Ethics' (Drew Lecture 1931, Independent Press, 1932).
[12] Packer, *art. cit.*, p.4.

question of urgency. In the early years of the modern missionary movement, this urgency was stated in terms of a certainty that those who in this life did not accept Jesus as Saviour would be damned. People were going to hell and they must be given their chance to believe in Jesus Christ. The matter was urgent. This way of stating the urgency of the evangelistic task is *now impossible for most.* . . . May I make bold to say that in our Christian churches the problem of unfaith lies precisely here, that, having lost confidence in the ways in which we used to state the necessity for evangelism, we have now ceased to believe in that necessity. We still believe that it is necessary for us to evangelize, but we do not believe that it is necessary for them to be evangelized. When our preaching does not convert we are concerned that we have failed, but there is little sense of loss concerning those who will not hear and believe.[13]

To show how this problem has percolated missionary thinking let me quote two articles from the *International Review of Missions* (July 1958). Both of these articles came from 'missionary statesmen' and while the first article is apologetic, the second is a spirited defence of the doctrine of universalism. Douglas Webster writes as follows:

> The most immediately powerful and straightforward missionary appeal today can be found with the Fundamentalist sects. Their impetus rests upon two ideas, sometimes fanatically and often exclusively grasped: hell and the Second Coming of our Lord. In former times both the Catholic and Protestant missions were motivated by fear of hell and all evangelical missions were inspired by the thought of hastening the Second Coming. We should not underestimate the appeal-potential of either of these notions. I remember as an undergraduate being most deeply moved by one of Amy Carmichael's books, *Things as they are.*

There follows the famous quotation where she pictures

[13] D. T. Niles, *The Preacher's Calling to be Servant* (Lutterworth, 1959), pp.32–33.

blind people pouring into the abyss, while Christians sit making daisy chains, with too few missionaries to guard the precipice. Universalism denies there is any precipice and any abyss. Then Webster continues:

> For myself I have to admit I still find this a very powerful picture. If we believe that men are going to burn eternally in hell unless they are converted to Christ before they die, there are many Christians who would go to all lengths to convert them. But the theological climate has changed. This is not to say that the doctrine of hell has been thrown overboard or that it is irrelevant to the Christian mission. It is some years now since Professor C. S. Lewis made hell respectable again, if one may put it like this. In any event the most formidable teaching about hell in the New Testament comes from the lips of our Lord Himself. We can neither ignore it nor reject it. But this is very different from believing that all the unconverted heathen perish everlastingly when they die. For most of us, this plank in the missionary appeal has forever been removed.[14]

In the second article H. D. Northfield helpfully distinguishes four groups of non-Christians: those who have wilfully rejected the gospel; those who have heard the gospel but not understood it; those who have so far had no opportunity to hear the gospel; and the vast majority who have lived and died without any opportunity of becoming acquainted with the gospel. It is with these 'legions of the ignorant' that the writer is concerned.

> But it is not too audacious to lay down the following proposition: that no infernal condition into which man may plunge himself is beyond the divine reach and that the categories of human punitive justice do not, in any way, apply to such cases. Hence it would seem, as far as we can understand, that only a small proportion of mankind is doomed to final punishment or annihilation. Not even those who definitely reject

[14] Douglas Webster, 'The Missionary Appeal Today', *IRM*, July 1958.

the grace of God are without hope, for so many of them 'know not what they do'.[15]

This view is also held by respected leaders in Third World churches:

> God's patient waiting for the soul's repentance must in the end be surely more potent than the soul's reluctance to repent and turn to Him (2 Pet. 3:9). The harmony of the heavenly worship would be impaired if, out of a hundred in the sheepfold, there is one soul which continues to languish in Sheol or 'the lake of fire'.[16]

It is this viewpoint which appears to underlie the present swing away from soteriological concern to social concern. Indeed, it is precisely because many leaders in the World Council of Churches believe that God will save all men anyway that ' "salvation" has been given such a firm this-worldly orientation'[17] and evangelism often becomes simply irrelevant.

The tenets of universalism

There is a wide spectrum of differing positions which may be described as universalistic in varying degrees, and not all of the tenets suggested below are necessarily found in combination. However, these attitudes do tend to hang together in an attempt to produce a coherent theological position. The following sections contain quotations to illustrate the theological position under review.

1. GOD IS A GOD OF LOVE AND SO THERE CAN BE NO HELL

The argument stems from the belief that because God is a God of love either there can be no hell at all, or people

---

[15] H. D. Northfield, 'The Legions of the Ignorant', *IRM*, July 1958, p.301.

[16] Professor John S. Mbiti quoted in *LTEHHV*, p.1222.

[17] N. T. Wright, 'Universalism and the World-Wide Community', *Churchman*, July–September 1975, p.204.

will not be permitted to stay there long. One example is enough:

> A theology based on sovereign love will uncompromisingly stand for universal salvation. Anything less would be inconsistent with God's sovereignty and would impune God's love . . . If He is sovereign love, the question as to the outcome is completely closed. Love will win unconditional surrender from all that is not love, and God will rule everywhere and forever.[18]

2. DIVINE SOVEREIGNTY MUST MEAN UNIVERSAL SALVATION

The fact that God is love and God is sovereign must inevitably ensure that all men will be saved. John Hick, for instance, assumes at the outset the very thing he will later seek to prove, namely that 'the eventual attainment of man's highest good is guaranteed by God's sovereignty: he has made his human creatures for fellowship with himself and will eventually bring them to this high end.'[19] There is a very attractive note of triumph in this so-called 'reformed universalism'. According to Romans 9 following, 'that is the final end of divine predestination and the ultimate triumph of divine will, that God coerces no-one and yet surrenders no-one, but wins them all. No-one will be forced, and even the stubborn heart will at length be overcome by the supreme revelation of the glory of God.'[20]

Again, Emil Brunner, who is very honest about the lack of biblical evidence for universalism, points out that this view of sovereignty 'when pushed to logical extremes leads to a doctrine of dual predestination'.[21]

Pushed to the other extreme it leads to the doctrine of universalism. What are our options here? Do we have to

[18] Nels Ferré, *The Christian Understanding of God* (Harper, 1951).

[19] John Hick, *Evil and the God of Love* (Fontana, 1968), p.17.

[20] Ethelbert Stauffer, *Theology of the New Testament* (SCM Press, 1955), p.231.

[21] E. Brunner, *Eternal Hope* (ET, Lutterworth, 1954), p.181.

choose between the doctrine of universalism on the one hand and the doctrine of particular redemption (that Christ died only for the elect) on the other? Tillich expresses the conflict:

> It presupposes an idea of predestination which actually excludes most human beings from eternal salvation and gives hope for salvation only to the few – comparatively few, even if it is millions – who are actually reached by the message of Jesus as the Christ. Such an idea is unworthy of the glory and the love of God and must be rejected in the name of the true relationship of God to his world.[22]

Does the stress on sovereignty force us to choose between universalism and hyper-Calvinism?

3. THE CROSS IS EFFECTIVE FOR ALL

'Reconciliation theology' is common today. Basically it claims that 'God has already won a mighty redemption ... for the entire world ... The task of the church is to tell all men ... that they already belong to Christ. ... Men are no longer lost.'[23] For its adherents, the message is this:

> I keep always in the foreground of my thought the fact that all those to whom I am privileged to speak about my Lord are already one with me in his saving ministry. I believe and confess him, they do not, and yet the essential facts of the gospel remain true for them as for me. God made us, God loves us, Jesus died for us, our trespasses are not counted, when we die we shall go to him who will be our judge. These affirmations are true of all men whether they know him or not, like them or not, accept them or not.[24]

---

[22] Paul Tillich, 'Mission and World History' in G. H. Anderson (ed.), *The Theology of the Christian Mission* (SCM Press, 1961), p.284.

[23] Dr Jitsuo Morikwa, Secretary of Evangelism of the American Baptist Convention.

[24] D. T. Niles, *Upon the Earth* (Lutterworth, 1962).

Critics of the view, however, are rather less euphoric in their appraisal of the teaching:

> The mission of the church is to announce to all men that their sins have already been forgiven, that their salvation has been accomplished by Christ's death, and that all they need to do is to accept forgiveness and salvation as the free gift of God. This makes it sound as if salvation could be had almost automatically. Evangelism then consists of informing people that they have already been saved, and of trying to persuade them to accept that notion.[25]

4. TRADITIONAL ORTHODOX TEACHING ON HELL IS IMMORAL AND REPULSIVE

There is a tendency here to caricature the full biblical picture and to present it as a chamber of horrors symbolizing eternal evil, a concentration camp in the midst of a blissful countryside, or as a heaven dependent upon other people not getting there. All of these criticisms are based on the 'equal and opposite' idea of hell,[26] whereas C. S. Lewis' view of hell as a minute place of shadows would seem more acceptable to tender consciences.[27] This 'aunt sally' about a repugnant view of hell is constantly being put up and knocked down. For the universalist, any morally sensitive and mature person must reject the idea of hell as being both sub-justice and sub-love. Indeed, 'that such a doctrine could be conceived, not to mention believed, shows how far from any understanding of the love of God many people once were and alas, still are.'[28] Even for those who can accept any idea of judgment, hell is real but temporary; a place where unbelievers can be

[25] Ilion T. Jones, 'Is Protestant Christianity being sabotaged from within?' *Christianity Today*, January, 1966.

[26] *Cf.* N. T. Wright, *art. cit.*, p.201.

[27] *Cf.* C. S. Lewis, *The Great Divorce* (Fontana, 1971).

[28] Nels Ferré, *The Atonement and Mission* (London Missionary Society, 1960).

brought to their senses. Hell does for unbelievers what in Roman theory purgatory does for believers.

5. BIBLICAL DESCRIPTIONS OF THE LAST JUDGMENT AND HELL ARE NOT DESCRIBING OBJECTIVE REALITY

In biblical eschatology such descriptions are related to facts only as a scientific formula or a model of an atom may be related to the real thing. They are not literal accounts of what will happen. What this boils down to is that biblical statements about judgment and hell are a kind of colourful threat, expressed in the only terms an intellectually and morally primitive kind of man can understand, in order to enable him to make the right decision about following God. The implication is that for modern man, in these more enlightened days, such colourful language is not required and that men will decide for God and heaven from more altruistic motives!

6. GOD SPEAKS THROUGH ALL RELIGIONS TO ALL PEOPLE

At the Nairobi assembly of the World Council of Churches in 1975 there was reference to 'the common search of people of various faiths, cultures and ideologies'. Universalism claims that God is too great and too noble to reveal himself in a single once-for-all revelation – God speaks in an infinite variety of ways through his common grace to mankind. 'Religion is essential to all and is God's call to his people. . . . There can no more be a Hindu, a Christian, or a Bahai medicine of immortality than there can be a Chinese, Aryan or Indian cure for cancer.'[29]

7. THE CHURCH HAS FAILED TO REACH ALL PEOPLE

Here, if we can sympathize with little else, we can share in the view expressed. Are people to be condemned because we missionaries have been slothful in our language study? Are people to perish everlastingly

[29] Nels Ferré.

because our exposition of the glories of the gospel has been inadequate or unattractive, or because we have failed to disentangle Christianity from Western culture? Humility makes us all shrink from that. Universalism measures the slow progress of missionary evangelism against an exploding world population – pagan populations are increasing at a geometric ratio. If the church is failing, then a loving, sovereign God must have another plan, the reasoning runs.

But this tenet of universalism contradicts some of the others. Why does a loving, sovereign God not stir up or revive the church so that it will effectively reach all people with the gospel? None the less this problem is one with which we must grapple. The powerlessness of the ecumenical 'gospel' in evangelism and church growth may lead them to excuse the people to whom they fail to preach. But all of us are faced with the agony of failing to communicate to non-Christians, so that the issue is a real one.

8. CHRISTIAN ECUMENISM LEADS LOGICALLY TO HUMAN ECUMENISM

The traditional emphasis of the WCC on the unity of the churches has largely given way to a concern about justice and liberation within humanity as a whole.

> The great issue of the hour is not Christian ecumenism but *human* ecumenism. Laudable as are the efforts of the World Council of Churches to bring some measure of understanding and charity into the relations of non-Roman Christian groups, the greater issue is practically untouched by that organization – namely, how to enter into a significant and mutually rewarding dialogue with the Asian faiths that are now beginning to show fresh life.[30]

Christians understand community on the basis of God's deal-

---

[30] Floyd H. Ross, 'The Christian Mission in Larger Dimension' in G. H. Anderson (ed.), *The Theology of the Christian Mission* (SCM Press, 1961).

ing with humanity in Jesus Christ. The Son of God, we believe, has assumed humanity on behalf of all people of all ages and cultures, and both authenticates and answers the basic human need for community. In him, God's love and purpose for salvation extend to all the corners of the earth.[31]

It can be seen very clearly that this identification of the church with the world and its universalistic assumptions lies behind all the WCC's enthusiasm for changing the structures of society and giving financial aid to buy arms for bloody revolution, massacre, atrocities, *etc.*

9. THERE IS A SECOND CHANCE AFTER DEATH

Here the argument is two-fold. First, that although the New Testament emphasizes the urgency of a decision for Christ here and now, it does not make death the great dividing line. And secondly, that to deny the possibility of salvation after death is to imply a limit and defect both in God's love and his power. There must therefore be some form of 'post mortem' encounter with Christ.

That the Bible mentions various forms of judgment after death is not disputed, but advocates of this position argue that this is remedial not punitive, leading more to a temporary purgatory than an eternal hell. The basic idea is that nobody is in hell because God wants them to be there, but of their own personal choice and that as soon as they repent and believe they may leave whenever they like. Whether there is any ground in Scripture for a belief of this kind is, of course, very much open to question. Again, if God's sovereign ability to call men effectually after death is posited, we have to ask why, if God wills to call them at all, he does not do it here. The speculative character of these arguments is obvious.

---

[31] *Jesus Christ Frees and Unites*, report from the Nairobi World Council of Churches, 1975, notes for Section 3.

10. THE BIBLE CAN BE MADE TO SUPPORT THE DOCTRINE OF UNIVERSALISM

This interpretation of Scripture must do two things. First, it must present those verses in the Bible which are capable of a universalistic interpretation and, secondly, it must provide an alternative explanation for, or demolish in other ways, those verses of Scripture which appear clearly to teach an ultimate and eternal division.

a. Verses capable of a universalistic interpretation fall into three main groups:

   i. Verses held to teach that the cross ensures universal salvation
       '. . . One died for *all*, therefore all died' (2 Cor. 5:14),
       ' . . . God was in Christ reconciling *the world* to Himself' (2 Cor. 5:19).
       ' . . . Through Him to reconcile *all things* to Himself' (Col. 1:20).
       ' . . . The grace of God has appeared, bringing salvation to *all men*' (Tit. 2:11).
       ' . . . By the grace of God He might taste death for *every one*' (Heb. 2:9).
       ' . . . Not for ours only, but also for those of the *whole world*' (1 Jn. 2:2).

   ii. Verses held to teach that God intends universal salvation
       ' . . . *All flesh* shall see the salvation of God' (Lk. 3:6).
       ' . . . Who desires *all men* to be saved and to come to the knowledge of the truth' (1 Tim. 2:4).
       ' . . . Not wishing for any to perish but for *all* to come to repentance' (2 Pet. 3:9).

   iii. Verses held explicitly to predict universal salvation
       ' . . . I, if I be lifted up from the earth, will draw *all men* to Myself' (Jn. 12:32).
       ' . . . The times of restoration (*apokatastasis*) of *all things*' (Acts 3:21).
       ' . . . Through one act of righteousness there resulted justification of life to *all men*' (Rom. 5:18).
       ' . . . For as in Adam all die, so also in Christ *all*

shall be made alive . . . then comes the end . . . when
all things are subjected to Him' (1 Cor. 15:22–28).

' . . . That *every tongue* should confess that Jesus
Christ is Lord' (Phil. 2:11).

' . . . we have fixed our hope on the living God, who
is the Saviour of *all men*' (1 Tim. 4:10).

*b. It is argued that the biblical expressions supporting the
doctrine of eternal punishment are pictorial and not
actual,* that the word 'eternal' as in 'eternal fire'
(Mt. 25:41) and 'eternal punishment' (Mt. 25:46), really
means the fire and punishment of 'the age'. But, similarly,
while the fire may not be quenched and the worm may
not die (Mk. 9:48) it is fire which continues and not that
which is consumed in it.

' . . . Until he should repay all that was owed him'
(Mt. 18:34).

' . . . And that slave who knew his master's will . . .
shall receive many lashes' (Lk. 12:47).

' . . . Until you have paid the very last cent' (Lk. 12:59).

'He is not the God of the dead, but of the living; for *all*
live to Him' (Lk. 20:38).

These verses are all interpreted in favour of the universalistic position. The genuineness of the parable of Dives
and Lazarus is questioned because a name appears in it,
and this man Lazarus is found in Abraham's bosom,
making it, so the argument goes, unlike any other parable
of Jesus. Such an apologetic is necessary from a universalistic understanding because the parable implies a permanent separation which cannot be terminated by those
who are suffering eternal torment. Equally clearly in this
parable is the fact that death is made the point of no
return.

The appeal of universalism

It cannot be denied that an assembly of arguments like
those given above and such a powerful group of proof
texts thrown in rapid succession are quite impressive. We
argue, naturally, that universalists must not so expound

these texts as to make them repugnant to those we quote; but of course they too may ask that we refrain from expounding texts in favour of eternal punishment in such a way as to be repugnant to the verses quoted in favour of the universalistic position – the more so, they would argue, as their scriptural arguments are backed up by general propositions drawn from the doctrine of God, and an ingrained human sense of justice. It is certainly true that such arguments, based upon the character of God, the apparent injustice of infinite punishment for a finite offence, and the impossibility of mothers being able to enjoy heaven while their children are still in hell, all have some intrinsic appeal.

The fatal weaknesses of universalism

Despite its attractiveness, universalism has many inherent weaknesses that make its tenability as a Christian doctrine extremely dubious and as a teaching of Jesus impossible.[32]

A theological position must be coherent. If it is not, then it should fail to gain our support. The adoption of universalism would seem to have the following consequences:

1. IT HAS A WEAK DOCTRINE OF SIN

There is no ultimate risk in the moral life. The wages of sin are at the most a temporary inconvenience rather than a danger of perdition. Judgment may be uncomfortable for a period but ultimate blessing is assured, however wicked the life lived. John Baillie says that universalism (which he espouses) must be stated in a form 'which does nothing to decrease the urgency of immediate repentance and which makes no promises to the procrastinating sinner. It is doubtful such a form of the doctrine has yet been found.'[33]

[32] J. Arthur Baird, *The Justice of God in the Teaching of Jesus* (SCM Press, 1963), p.230.
[33] John Baillie, *And the Life Everlasting* (OUP, 1934), p.245.

2. IT HAS AN EASY CONCEPT OF SALVATION

Salvation is not a matter of life and death but of 'sooner' or 'later'. There is no special urgency about entering salvation – there will always be plenty more chances later on.

3. IT OFFENDS THE LOGIC OF THE CROSS

If salvation is more a matter of convenience than a matter of life and death, the cross seems to lose its necessity and to be too drastic a remedy for such a situation.

4. IT OFFENDS THE FREEDOM OF MAN'S WILL

Baird pictures God 'dragging unrepentant sinners screaming into heaven' because men are 'doomed to be saved' (the title of a 19th century tract), whether they want to or not.[34] Many universalists would suggest that men finally respond to the love of God of their own free will. But what kind of free will is it which in the long run *must* choose bliss? Any appearance of genuine freedom to choose on earth is lost by 'third degree' applied in hell – clearly any sensible fellow will choose heaven.

5. IT REMOVES ANY URGENCY FROM GOSPEL PREACHING AND MISSIONARY ENDEAVOUR

If all men are to be saved in the end why bother to urge men to repent now? They will later in any case. Why bother to be converted oneself for that matter? But the urgency which has characterized missionary endeavour derives not merely from the fear of hell, but from the consciousness that to live even this life without Christ is to be condemned to an alienated, meaningless existence estranged from God.

[34] J. A. Baird, *op. cit.*, p.221.

6. IT IGNORES THE BIBLICAL STRESS ON THE DECISIVENESS OF THIS LIFE AND ITS DECISIONS

Why did Jesus warn the Jews that the issue of unbelief would be that they would die in their sins (John 8:21, 24)? . . . Why did he include in the story of Dives and Lazarus the detail about the great gulf fixed between those in joy and those in torment (Luke 16:26)? None of these statements is explicable save on the basis that, for better or for worse, the choices and commitments made in this life have abiding consequences for the life to come, and he who does not lay hold of life here will certainly not enjoy it hereafter.[35]

7. IT CONDEMNS THE PREACHING OF CHRIST AND HIS APOSTLES AS EITHER INEPT OR IMMORAL

Again Packer expresses this much better than I can:

Evangelicals have sometimes been censured for preaching hell and the wrath to come, and counselling their hearers to flee from it, and so avoid a lost eternity. But Jesus and the apostles did the same! Now, if universalism is true, and the founders of Christianity did not know it, their preaching stands revealed as ignorant and incompetent; and if universalism is true, and they did know it, their preaching stands as a bluff, frightening people into the kingdom by holding before them unreal terrors.[36]

The doctrine of universalism is a 'Trojan Horse': it may have a venerable pedigree (as a heresy) *but its aim is the overthrow of the church militant. Such an interpretation makes nonsense of a great deal of the New Testament.* Why did Paul and the other apostles go through such suffering in order to reach men and women with the gospel? Why were men willing to lay down their lives rather than recant and offer incense to the false gods of Rome? If pardon could have been obtained immediately on entrance into the other

---

[35] J. I. Packer, *art. cit., Bibliotheca Sacra*, 130 (January 1973), p.13.
[36] *Ibid.*, p.13.

world, where in any case they would have been joined shortly by their persecutors, it must all seem like a terrible mistake. But a doctrine which inevitably makes all the heroes and martyrs of the Christian church appear misguided is surely suspect.

Refutation of the tenets of univeralism

1. GOD IS A GOD OF LOVE

This is perfectly true. But does it therefore follow that there can be no hell or no eternal punishment?

> A good many false conclusions may be founded upon the phrase 'God is love'. For instance, one may say, 'God is love, and He will not allow sin with its terrible consequences to continue in the world' and yet sin is rampant everywhere. Again, 'God is love, and He will not allow wrong to triumph over right' and yet men have seen through all ages and in all places wrong openly victorious over right. Again, 'God is love, and He will not allow His creatures to suffer.' And yet from the beginning the whole creation has groaned in pain, waiting to be delivered.[37]

While Northfield may argue that 'we cannot state what He will do or not do; save only that He, being the Father of our Lord Jesus Christ, will love. The resources of such infinite love are infinite too',[38] this begs the whole question. Certainly *we* cannot state what God will do or not do, but we can state what *God* has stated he will do or not do. Christian integrity forbids us to state or suggest anything else. If God has told us what he will do – revealing his will to us in the Bible, given us for just this purpose – what folly it is to ignore what *God* has stated he *will* do, in favour of what *we* suppose he *might* do! We set aside what claims to be the Word of God, in favour of what we know to be the word of man. 'To foist attributes on God

---

[37] H. W. Frost, *The Spiritual Condition of the Heathen*, p.5.
[38] H. D. Northfield, *art. cit., IRM*, July 1958, p.304.

– particularly such an attribute as the peculiarly modern notion of a love incompatible with sternness or serious judgment – is neither safe nor wise.'[39]

It is not as though a God of love has not already acted to deliver men and women from the penalty of hell and punishment.

> In the long run the answer to all those who object to the doctrine of hell is itself a question: 'What are you asking God to do?' To wipe out their past sins and, at all costs, to give them a fresh start, smoothing every difficulty and offering every miraculous help? But He has done so, on Calvary. To forgive them? They will not be forgiven. To leave them alone? Alas, I am afraid that is what He does.[40]

The co-existence of hell with the God of love would seem a moral necessity if man is to have freedom of choice. We know all too sadly even in human experience that love may be rejected and that a person may persist in wilful hatred and estrangement, even when it is not in his interests to do so. Human pride can keep a man in hell.

2. DIVINE SOVEREIGNTY

Those with an Arminian background, eager to argue that Calvary is sufficient for all, may find that in fleeing from universalism their only refuge is in the adoption of limited atonement (particular redemption), a step, however, which they fear would drive them to a doctrine of double predestination. It is a problem capable of no facile solution. The Christian mind must ever seek to wrestle to understand the revealed truth of God, yet at the same time to be able to recognize the limitations of human understanding. We take the Bible as our sufficient guide, believing what it says, neither more nor less. If we find there God's clear warnings that men may be lost, may perish, may be cast into outer darkness, into eternal fire

[39] N. T. Wright, *art. cit.*, *Churchman*, July–September 1975, p.201.
[40] C. S. Lewis, *The Problem of Pain* (Fontana, 1940), p.116.

and eternal punishment, then, what right have we to overthrow what Christ has taught by philosophizing about matters which our minds cannot grasp? There is surely a difference between 'willing', in the sense of desiring all mankind to be saved, and 'decreeing' that all men should be saved or that some should be saved and some lost.[41]

3. THE CROSS IS EFFECTIVE FOR ALL

Michael Green points out that in 2 Corinthians 5:20, 'Paul beseeches his readers to be "reconciled with God", proof positive that their reconciliation, in our sense of that word, was not yet complete, although God had been in Christ *katallassōn* the world unto himself.'[42] The reconciliation is not automatic; there are two parties to a reconciliation (as indicated in Article II of the Church of England which says 'Christ died to reconcile his Father to us'). God has been reconciled to us – in fact it was he who took these wonderful steps to effect this reconciliation through the Lord Jesus Christ – but now we have to exhort *men* to be reconciled to God. The cross is sufficient for all, but efficient only for those who will be reconciled and make the necessary response of repentance and faith. The constant emphasis of Scripture is that the gospel 'is the power of God for salvation to every one who *believes*' (Rom. 1:16). The power of Christ is like a locomotive full of power and ready to carry us forward. Man is powerless to move himself one inch toward heaven; the coupling of faith is essential if he is to be saved. 'He who believes in Him is not judged; he who does not believe has been judged already' (Jn. 3:18). The cross without faith is like a vaccine without a syringe.

---

[41] See Edwin A. Blum, 'Shall you not surely die?' *Themelios*, January 1979.
[42] E. M. B. Green, *The Meaning of Salvation* (Hodder, 1965), p.227.

4. THE DOCTRINE OF HELL IS IMMORAL AND REPULSIVE

It could be argued that sin also is repulsive, and that an arms merchant or slave dealer deserves a hell which is very repulsive indeed. But the chief question is: 'repulsive to whom?' Not to Jesus, who taught it so evidently. 'It would contradict the whole Gospel tradition about Jesus to refer to the severity of the later church, the conception – so odious to modern man – of an ultimate discrimination.'[43] We should notice that the only references to Gehenna and Hades in the New Testament are found on the lips of Jesus. The words are not used by any other New Testament speaker or writer (except for a poorly-attested reading for 'grave' in 1 Cor. 15:55). The only one who can speak with authority is one who has himself come down from heaven and who is the incarnate Son of God. It is significant that if we deny this doctrine we are denying a doctrine which was taught by Jesus himself. If we try to attribute this to the severity of the later church it is puzzling to know why that church made no such reference in other writings, but included it in the teaching of Jesus.

We are familiar with the idea that a 'definite choice' (*e.g.* of a life partner) may have pleasant or unpleasant consequences of considerable duration. Small choices which prove to be wrong may invite terrible consequences for many people, apparently out of all proportion to the original mistake. In this case an act of repentance and turning in faith to accept the Lord Jesus as Saviour brings eternal blessing (no-one objects to that!); and it does not seem unreasonable that the failure to take this step should also have eternal consequences. Surely wilful defiance of an eternal God is bound to bring eternal misery! What right has a finite intellect to question the infinite will of God?

[43] Emil Brunner, *Eternal Hope*, p.177.

5. BIBLICAL LANGUAGE DOES NOT EXPRESS OBJECTIVE REALITIES

So the Bible gives pictures of reality rather than reality itself. The semantic problem of expressing in human language that which falls outside human experience is humbly recognized; this, after all, is what a great deal of modern theological controversy is all about. There is a real problem in the use of human language to express divine truth. None the less biblical language has been given to us by God himself in order to convey meaning, and the words used do indicate reality.

Moreover, on some occasions Christ speaks in explanation of a parable or allegory (*e.g.* in the parable of the tares, when in explaining the significance of the tares Jesus speaks of coming realities). He does not use parabolic language in explaining parables. 'The Son of Man will send forth His angels, and they will gather out of His kingdom all stumbling blocks, and those who commit lawlessness, and will cast them into the furnace of fire; in that place there shall be weeping and gnashing of teeth' (Mt. 13:41–42).

Unless we are to evacuate biblical words of all meaning (in which case we have no foundation for any faith or any theology at all) we must accept the words of our Lord Jesus Christ as meaning what they say. Consuming fire and outer darkness are comprehensible in their fearsomeness and dread.

6. GOD SPEAKS THROUGH ALL RELIGIONS TO ALL PEOPLE

This would not seem to be a fair statement of the Bible's teaching about other religions, which are seen variously as humanly devised imaginations (Rom. 1:21–23), worship of demons (1 Cor. 10:20), or worship of graven images, an abomination to the Lord, to be utterly detested and abhorred and burnt with fire (Dt. 7). The Old Testament attitude towards other religions was well known by our Lord Jesus, who never repudiated it.

It is repeatedly urged that as God is at work in history and in the world in general, so he is also at work in other religions.[44]

More recently the idea of 'anonymous Christians' has been suggested by Karl Rahner. This is scarcely a biblical view of religion in either the Old or the New Testament and the concept has been very amusingly shot down by Hans Küng:

> Does this solve the problem? Are the masses of the non-Christian religions really marching in to the holy Roman Church or is this going on only in the theologian's head? Anyway, in reality, they – Jews, Muslims, Hindus, Buddhists, and all the others, who know quite well that they are 'unanonymous' – remain outside. Nor have they any wish to be inside. . . . And it would be impossible to find anywhere in the world the sincere Jew, Muslim or atheist who would not regard the assertion that he is an 'anonymous' Christian as presumptuous. To bring the partner to the discussion into our own circle in this way closes the dialogue before it has even begun. This is a pseudo-solution which offers slight consolation. Is it possible to cure a society suffering from a decline in membership by declaring that even non-members are 'hidden' members? But what would Christians say if they were graciously recognized by Buddhists as 'anonymous' Buddhists?[45]

The Jewish religion was given by revelation of the God of Christianity, yet Paul agonized for the salvation of his people. There is no trace of the notion that proselytization must be avoided and their religion respected. The Jews are told: 'Repent, and . . . be baptized in the name of Jesus Christ' (Acts 2:38); that there is salvation in no-one

---

[44] See, for example, the famous book by Raymond Panikkar, *The Unknown Christ of Hinduism* (Darton, Longman & Todd, 1965).
[45] Hans Küng, *On being a Christian* (Collins, 1977), p.98.

136

else (Acts 4:12) and that 'through him everyone who believes is freed from all things, from which you could not be freed through the Law of Moses' (Acts 13:39). The Lord Jesus himself spoke to Jews about heaven and judgment.

When Paul arrived in Athens he regarded even the Athenians as ignorant idolaters. Philosophy could not save men who were facing judgment (Acts 17:31). Their multiplicity of altars was wrong (Acts 17:29) and the only hope of 'all men everywhere' was that they should repent (Acts 17:30).

It is impossible to find support in the New Testament for peaceful co-existence with other religions; there is only one revealed truth, found in the Scriptures of the Old and New Testaments. How can Buddhism, which denies creation, the existence of evil and moral responsibility, peaceably co-exist with Christianity? How can Islam which also calls on the God of Abraham and expects Jesus to come in judgment, and yet denies the person and work of Christ, be seen as an equal with Christianity? Anyone who denies these truths is a false prophet.

Confusion between creation and redemption is fundamental to these current false views. It is fascinating in this context, therefore, to read the words of Paul Tillich, who is not normally regarded as theologically conservative!

Moreover, missions is not an attempt to unite the different religions. If this were the function of missions, a uniting point, or center, would have to exist. Then, however, *this* uniting center would be the center of history and the Christ would become 'decentralized'. He would no longer be the center; but the center would be that which is above him and also above Buddha, Mohammed and Confucius. The Christian Church would then be *one* religious group among others, but it would not be the agency of the kingdom of God, as we have described it and as it has always felt itself to be . . . Is Christianity the absolute religion? Is Christ the center of history? Is he the bringer of the New Being? Or are the other religions of equal value and does each culture have its own proper religion? According to these ideas, Christianity belongs to the Western world and it should not interfere with the religious developments of the Eastern world. This, of course, would deny the claim that Jesus is the Christ, the bringer of the New Being. It would make this statement obsolete, because he who brings the New Being is not a relative figure but an absolute figure, an all-embracing figure.[46]

We must accept the sincerity of the beliefs of others and we may recognize that as well as biblical Judaism almost in its totality there are aspects in the ethics of Buddhism and most certainly in the prayerfulness of Islam which we can deeply appreciate. But we cannot adopt the 'fruit salad' syncretistic approach which seems favoured by some. In an earlier chapter we have made it clear that the Western or Anglo-Saxon cultural accretions must be shed as the Christian faith becomes indigenous in each new culture. But the essential doctrinal core of Christian faith cannot be modified without it ceasing to be Christian.

7. THE FAILURE OF THE CHURCH TO REACH OTHERS

We confess this to our shame and wish that all Christian churches felt the same burden and concern to reach the unreached. But to argue that God's justice is in some way affected by the great numbers who remain untouched by the gospel is to beg the question. God is just whether he allows only one person or untold numbers the consequences of unbelief. The situation is tragic, but the principles remain unchanged.[47]

We do not know if God has any alternative plan. We do not know on what basis people who have lived before Christ or before the message of Christ was brought to them may have any hope of salvation. Paul Tillich points out that 'many people, even today, are still living *before*

[46] Paul Tillich in *The Theology of the Christian Mission*, pp.284–285.
[47] H. W. Frost, *The Spiritual Condition of the Heathen*, p.5.

the event of Jesus as the Christ; others, those who have accepted Jesus as the Christ, are living *after* the center of history.'[48]

We know that God judged Sodom and Gomorrah, and had mercy on the people of Nineveh when they repented. We know that people like Melchizedek and the wise men appear in the Bible record almost out of the blue, while God speaks to and through men like Abimelech and Balaam. But there is too little here on which to build a doctrine of syncretism. What we do have is the command to make disciples of *all nations;* and we have the gospel to preach to them: a command to *all men* everywhere to repent (Acts 17); and we have the responsibility to teach them *all the things* which Christ taught us, and that includes the facts of judgment, heaven and hell (Mt. 28:20).

8. HUMAN ECUMENISM

The Bible repeatedly divides men into two categories, and the teaching of Jesus does this incessantly. The parables 'all express the thought of judgment', says Emil Brunner. Sheep and goats, tares and wheat, good fish and bad, fruitful and unfruitful, profitable and slothful, wise and foolish, the way to life and the way to destruction – what biblical grounds can be found for ultimately bringing together things which the Bible teaches will ultimately be separated?

'In this century, however, exegesis has turned decisively against the universalist cure. Few would now doubt that many NT texts clearly teach a *final* division of mankind into saved and lost'.[49]

9. A SECOND CHANCE

It would be a relief to believe in this, and comforting to be able to say so at the funerals of unbelievers. But on

[48] Tillich, *art. cit.*, p. 283.
[49] Richard J. Bauckham, 'Universalism: a Historical Survey', *Themelios,* January 1979, p.52.

what authority? The whole idea is quite gratuitous and we have no right to make such unjustified additions to biblical revelation. What we know is what God has told us, and no more. If the Bible tells us that 'it is appointed for men to die once, and after this comes judgment' (Heb. 9:27) what right have we to add to this 'and after that release'? Quite apart from the results of teaching of this kind, as we have already seen, there is not a shred of evidence for it in the Bible. If God is sovereignly able to call men effectually after death, then one must ask why God does not call them effectually now?

10. THE BIBLICAL EVIDENCE

To examine all these texts thoroughly in their contexts would take far more space than is available here.[50] It is worth making some brief general observations, however.

a. 'All the texts admit of other explanations more germane to their context.'[51]

b. The word 'all' need not necessarily imply universality, but 'all of some sorts' and 'some of all sorts'. Thus, for example, Romans 10:11–13 and 11:32 show from their context that 'all' means all races and not necessarily all individuals. Green suggests in one instance: 'The writer may be attacking the exclusiveness of a proto-Gnostic heresy which was restricting salvation to a particular class.'[52]

c. In New Testament Greek the word 'saviour' was used in the sense of 'preserver' or 'Lord Protector' as a title of the Roman emperors and the normal use of the word 'save' meant 'to make safe' or 'preserve'. This seems to be the usage in Philippians 3:20 with a comparison of the

[50] For this, we may see the relevant commentaries, E. M. B. Green's helpful examination of the texts in *The Meaning of Salvation.* J. I. Packer's treatment in his article in *Bibliotheca Sacra,* 130, January 1973, and most recently N. T. Wright's 'Towards a Biblical View of Universalism' in *Themelios,* January 1979. pp. 225–230.

[51] Packer, *art. cit.,* p.7.

[52] Green, *op. cit.,* p.229.

citizenship and 'protectorship' of Rome and of heaven. It would seem probable that 1 Timothy 2:3–4 and 4:10 have a similar meaning.

d. Many texts are accompanied by statements which can only mean that finally some do perish. To interpret these texts from a universalist perspective is 'to accuse New Testament writers, and indeed the Lord himself, of intellectual schizophrenia!'[53]

e. It is a little amusing to notice the reliance placed upon texts from the pastoral epistles by those who otherwise contend that they represent a tradition later than primitive Christianity!

f. Wright comments that some advocates of universalism still attempt to argue their case from certain passages in the Pauline corpus. 'An odd inversion, this, of the old liberal position where Jesus was the teacher of heavenly truths and Paul the cross-grained dogmatic bigot.'[54] It is the 'hard sayings' of Jesus himself which warn most clearly of eternal punishment.

Emil Brunner in spite of his own universalistic leanings is very clear on the weakness of the biblical evidence, and speaks of

> ... the attempt to qualify all affirmations about the last judgment by making the latter an interim affair after which alone that which is truly ultimate will come. Hence the expressions by which the New Testament emphasizes apparently the finality of the last judgment and of the damnation of the reprobate are so interpreted as to impart to judgment the character of a transitional stage, of a pedagogic cleansing process. *Aiōnios* does not mean eternal, but only eschatological; the inextinguishable fire, the worm that dies not, the destruction, the second death, *etc.*, all these quite unequivocal expressions in themselves are subjected to such a protracted process of exegetical chemistry that they lose the definiteness of their ultimate character. The means of this exegetical chem-

---

[53] Packer, *op. cit.*, p.7.
[54] N. T. Wright, 'Towards a Biblical View of Universalism', p.55.

istry do not stand the test of conscientious examination; we have here evasion rather than exegesis.[55]

Wright further hammers this home when he says,

> Of these objections the best known, and still the most powerful, is the presence in the Gospels – on the lips of Jesus himself – of sayings which leave no room whatsoever for the universalist position. The sheep and the goats, the separation of the rich man and Lazarus, the broad and narrow ways, the fate of those who cause little ones to stumble – these and many many more are clear and uncompromising.[56]

The universalist, therefore, has to argue *either* that the biblical verses do not mean what they say, *or* that they do not preclude a second chance and a later opening of the gates of hell, *or* that they have an existential meaning calculated to bring the hearer to a sense of his need for decision! The teaching of the Lord Jesus Christ seems to be quite plain – men are continually warned of the perils of sin and consequent judgment, and urged to flee from destruction. If the sayings of Jesus are at least more or less correctly reported and if universalism is true, then we must condemn the preaching of Christ and his apostles as either inept or immoral, for

> . . . if universalism is true, and the founders of Christianity did not know it, their preaching stands revealed as ignorant and incompetent; and if universalism is true, and they did know it, their preaching stands revealed as a bluff, frightening people into the kingdom by holding before them unreal terrors. I leave it to the universalists to choose which of these options to settle for.[57]

---

[55] Emil Brunner, *Eternal Hope*, p.183.
[56] N. T. Wright, 'World-Wide Community', p.202.
[57] Packer, *art. cit.*, p.10.

Conclusion

It looks then as though we must consider universalism to be a latter-day version of Satan's lie to Eve, 'Thou shalt not surely die'.[58] If universalism has already been condemned by the church, and if its conclusions are as damaging as has been suggested, then it must be resisted. Of course we gladly proclaim the wonder of God's lovingkindness, patience and mercy to us sinners, but we must at the same time declare the dread consequences of exercising our human freedom to refuse cleansing and new creation when God offers it to us in the gospel.

When we turn from the world and its idols to serve the living and the true God we are brought into the fellowship of his people, the church. If we escape God's judgment upon the world, it is by entering the ark of his church. We must not confuse God's concern for the world with his calling his church out of it (*ekklēsia*). Any ecumenical attempt to effect a merger between the church and the world is to confuse what God distinguishes and to attempt vainly to unite what God is determined to divide.

Material for study

Douglas Webster, 'The Missionary Appeal Today', *IRM*, July 1958.

H. D. Northfield, 'The Legions of the Ignorant', *IRM*, July 1958.

N. T. Wright, 'Universalism and the World-Wide Community', *Churchman*, July – September 1975, vol. 89 No. 3.

Richard J. Bauckham, 'Universalism: a Historical Survey', *Themelios*, January 1979, Vol. 4 No. 2.

Questions for discussion

1. 'God's concern, which presumably the Christian should share, is the world and not the church' (J. G. Davies). Discuss.
2. Does God intend to save the world or the church?
3. Why does liberal theology draw the conclusions of universal

---

[58] *Cf.* Packer, *art. cit.*, p.5.

salvation from sovereignty, while conservative theology derives the doctrine of an ultimate division from human freedom? Is this the biblical way round?

4. Does the view that all men will be saved encourage or discourage missionary motivation?

5. Do we see the reign of God in Diocletian's Rome, the British empire, Nazi Germany, Stalin's Russia, the United States or the New China? If so, in what sense, and how does this relate to the position of the church in these states?

5 The grace of God for planting and perfecting churches

At first sight this may seem a strange subject to include in a book on mission. But just as we have seen that as regards the *ends* of mission and church building we have become *program*-orientated instead of *goal*-orientated, so also in relation to the *means* of mission we have tended to become *method*-orientated rather than *grace*-orientated.

This tendency in ecclesiology to substitute modern methodology and technology for the 'grace and power' orientation of the New Testament is not restricted to Americans, though they have been the greatest exponents of it. As Padilla points out rather pungently:

> For this, the twentieth century has provided it with the perfect tool – technology. The strategy for the evangelization of the world thus becomes a question of mathematical calculation. The problem is to produce the greatest number of Christians at the least possible cost in the shortest possible time, and for this the strategists can depend on the work of the computer. Thanks to computers, never in the modern era have we been closer to the re-establishment of one culture unified by the Christian faith – the *Corpus Christianum*, the 'culture Christianity of our day' has at its disposal the most sophisticated technological resources to propagate its message of success throughout the world and to do it *efficiently*![1]

[1] René Padilla, 'Evangelism and the World', *LTEHHV*, p.26.

The problem is that we reduce the gospel to a formula for success. The triumph of Christ becomes the obtaining of the highest number of conversions. Christianity becomes man-centred, conditioned by a 20th century 'technological mentality'. Padilla claims that this obsession with finding the 'one best way' in evangelism is just another form of worldliness.

It is this 'fierce pragmatism' that thinks primarily in terms of methodology – 'How to work for Christ', 'How to lead a soul to Christ', 'the Four Spiritual Laws', 'How to organize a Gospel Blimp, a Gospel Boat' *etc.* One Bible school taught how to deliver a gospel bullet – a rolled tract delivered by an automobile travelling at a defined speed, at a fixed distance from the curb, *etc.* (seriously!).

Anglican pastoralia teaches us 'How to conduct a marriage, a funeral, a baptism' and (does this astonish you? Whole schools of thought exist on the subject) 'How (or how not) to conduct a communion service'!

We tend to substitute temporal, program-orientated *ends for spiritual and biblical ends.* We also tend to substitute human and methodological *means* for spiritual *means.* In the matter of 'why and where' we substitute a human programme and human organization for the divine goals of a divine institution. Similarly in the matter of 'how' we have a similar tendency to depend on human efforts and human power rather than upon the 'grace and power' orientation of the New Testament.

If it be understandably protested that we have not totally ignored the spiritual, that can be granted. But we have tended to confine such discussion of what we regard as a *devotional* matter to the *chapel*, rather than treating it as a *doctrinal* matter which is a proper subject for the *classroom*! It is thought to be somehow unfair and unsporting to bring the 'supernatural' into the sphere of 'scholarship'! It is surely time this absurd dichotomy was ended. If the Bible has a good deal to say about *grace and power* as the means by which the early church obtained its goals, then these continue to be a proper subject for biblical scholarship. We must not relegate worship and God's grace and power from the classroom to the chapel. There is a quotation in J. S. Whale somewhere about our propensity for 'discussing theories of the atonement rather than falling down before the wounds of Christ and worshipping'.

So I make no further apology for insisting that this is a crucial question for mission. In earlier chapters we have been trying to discuss biblically what God's goals for the church really are. Surely it is also important to determine *how* God intends us to attain these goals, to discover, that is, God's means!

I have written elsewhere on the subject of spiritual gifts,[2] but in this chapter I want to approach the same subject from the opposite end. There I tried to discover what the spiritual gifts are and how they are to be obtained; here we begin with our goal of *quantitative church growth*, the multiplication of individuals and of congregations and ask '*How*'? The New Testament means would seem to be the gift of *evangelists* to win converts, and *apostles* to found new churches. When we think about *qualitative church growth* of the kind discussed in the first chapter, we need the gifts of *prophecy, teaching, encouraging, etc.* in order to build up the church (*i.e.* for 'edification'). For 'organization' we need the spiritual gifts of administration (*kubernēsis*), leaders (*proistamenoi*), and helps (*antilēmpsis*, probably financial). For worship other spiritual gifts would seem relevant ('each one has a psalm, has a teaching', *etc.*, 1 Cor. 14:26). The gifts of healing, miracles and exorcism may have an important evidential value in cross-cultural penetration. It may also provoke discussion to consider how and whether gifts of 'language' and 'interpretation' may not properly be related to the problem of communication in cross-cultural situations. In other words I want to consider *charismata* as the divine

---

[2] *Cinderella's Betrothal Gifts* (OMF, 1978).

method whereby mission is carried out and the church built up.

Grace and power

We meet an exciting description of early church activity when we read 'and with *great power* the apostles were giving witness to the resurrection of the Lord Jesus and *abundant grace* was upon them all' (Acts 4:33). This same combination appears later in describing Stephen as 'full of *grace and power*, . . . performing great wonders and signs among the people' (Acts 6:8).

It is very easy in English translations of the Bible to overlook the obvious relationship between *charis* and the clearly derived word *charisma (charismata* in the plural). This relationship between grace and gifts is too obvious to be accidental, as is clear from the following key passages about gifts:

Rom. 12:6   'Since we have *charismata* that differ according to the *charis* given to us . . .'

1 Pet. 4:10   'As each one has received a *charisma*, employ it . . . as good stewards of the manifold *charis* of God.'

1 Cor. 1:4–5,7   'I thank my God always concerning you, for the *charis* of God which was given you in Christ Jesus, that in everything you were enriched in Him, in all speech and all knowledge . . . so that you are not lacking in any *charisma*.'

While the word *charismata* is not used in Ephesians, it is also in the context of gifts (*domata*) that we read 'but to each one of us *charis* was given . . .' (Eph. 4:7). This relationship is clear in German where spiritual gifts are called *Gnadegabe*, literally 'grace-gifts'. It is as though the grace of God shines upon the prism of the congregation and is refracted into a spectrum of 'grace-gifts'. Gifts are not so much personal attributes or acquisitions as outpourings of God's grace.

Charismata means the results of grace. God's grace is

148

ministered to the congregation and manifested through spiritual gifts. Thus John Goldingay defines *charisma* as 'God's grace finding particular and concrete actualization'.[3] We notice that the origin of a *charisma* does not lie in the person who exercises it, but derives directly from the pouring of God's grace upon the congregation.

We have been so preoccupied with 'grace', in the form of God's *common grace* to all mankind and particularly his *saving grace* to all believers, that we very readily overlook this quite different usage of the word grace which we might call *serving grace* or *congregational grace*. This concept throws a great deal of light upon other Scriptures. For example (and very relevant to our subject), when missionaries were sent out 'they had been commended to the *grace of God* for the work' (Acts 14:26; *cf.* 15:40). Moreover, when those missionaries leave behind a newly planted church they commend its members 'to God and to the word of *His grace*, which is able to build you up . . .' (Acts 20:32).

This need for *charis* in his 'charismatic' ministry is repeatedly made evident in Paul's own descriptions of it. Thus, 'We have received *grace* and apostleship' (Rom. 1:5); it is 'according to the *grace* of God which was given to me, as a wise master builder' that Paul laid the foundation of the church in Corinth (1 Cor. 3:10). He is able to say that 'by the grace of God I am what I am, and His grace toward me did not prove vain; but I laboured even more than all of them, yet not I, but the *grace* of God with me' (1 Cor. 15:10). It is the 'stewardship of God's *grace* which was given to me for you . . . of which I was made a minister, according to the gift of God's *grace* which was given to me according to the working of His power. To me, the very least of all saints, this *grace* was given, to preach to the Gentiles the unfathomable riches of Christ' (Eph. 3:2,7,8).

[3] John Goldingay, *The Church and the Gifts of the Spirit* (Grove Books, 1972), p.5.

There are other familiar verses where this understanding of 'serving grace' may throw light:

> Let the word of Christ richly dwell within you, with all wisdom, teaching and admonishing one another with psalms and hymns and spiritual songs (*en tē chariti*), singing in your hearts to the Lord (Col. 3:16).

> You therefore, my son, be strong in the *grace* which is in Christ Jesus. And the things which you have heard from me in the presence of many witnesses, these entrust to faithful men who will be able to teach others also (2 Tim. 2:1–2).

The latter is a reference to grace in connection with the teaching ministry, one of the most commonly referred to of the *charismata*. This may also throw light on the injunction to 'grow in grace' (2 Pet. 3:18) and on the entreaty 'not to receive the grace of God in vain' (2 Cor. 6:1).

We also realize that the child Jesus grew up, 'and the grace of God was upon Him' (Lk. 2:40). When at the beginning of his ministry he spoke in the synagogue, they wondered at the 'words of grace which proceeded out of his mouth' (Lk. 4:22). This understanding of grace also gives a further dimension to our understanding of John 1:16: 'For of His fulness we have all received, and grace upon grace.'

In our first chapter we thought of the immediate goals of church and mission and in our last chapter we are to think of the ultimate long-term goal. But it seems clear that the *means* by which these goals are to be attained are not methods and techniques, however well tried and tested and perfected, but a humble reliance on that same grace and power ministered to us by the Holy Spirit. We too-readily rely on methods rather than on God.

If, in our ministry, we are to see the church grow both quantitatively and qualitatively, whether in this country or overseas, then we will have to experience 'great power' and 'abundant grace'.

A spectrum of charismata

Some individuals manifestly exercise more than one gift. Paul and Barnabas are both listed among the 'prophets and teachers' in Antioch (Acts 13:1); yet both are shortly afterwards called 'apostles' (Acts 14:14). When Barnabas first appears (Acts 4:36–37) he is exercising the gift of giving (Rom. 12:8), while his nickname reminds us that he is an outstanding example of the gift of encouragement (Rom. 12:8). Paul also manifested on occasion the gift of healing and miracles and apparently claimed the gift of languages. Thus each exercised at least five different gifts.

Even more confusing is the fact that not only may one individual fulfil several functions, but the biblical definitions themselves merge into one another and overlap. Rather than reading as distinct gifts:

APOSTLE PROPHET TEACHER SHEPHERD

there appears a continuous spectrum:

APOSTLEPROPHETEACHERSHEPHERD

This overlap is implied when the Antioch church leaders are described as 'prophets and teachers' without saying which are which, and suggesting that all five were both. In Ephesians 4:11 the absence of the article before 'teachers' indicates that 'pastor/teachers' are a single group.[4] Silas, who together with Timothy was included with Paul as 'apostles of Christ' (1 Thes. 2:6), is described as a 'prophet' (Acts 15:32) when he is said to have 'encouraged and strengthened the brethren with a lengthy message'. So a prophet, in fulfilling his ministry, exercises the gift of encouragement. While it is true that words like prophet, teacher, encourager, pastor, or evangelist each have their own distinctive shade of meaning, both teaching and encouraging, for example, are part of the prophetic function. He is a poor evangelist who does no teaching. The effective church-founding apostle must also engage in

---

[4] It is possible that the phrase 'apostles and prophets' in Eph. 2:20 and 3:5 may be a similar type of overlap.

evangelism, teaching and encouraging, which are essential parts of his apostolic task.

The gifts of grace appear like a spectrum; each colour may be distinguished from others as distinctively violet, blue, indigo, *etc.*, at its centre, but each merges into the adjacent colours at its edges. Each gift has its own distinctive purpose, but overlaps with neighbouring gifts. No one individual displays the whole spectrum of the gifts of God's manifold grace (though Paul must have approached it), but one individual may possess several related gifts.

We are about to observe that apostles are always evangelizing and that any biblical definition of prophecy is bound to include some aspects of teaching. It is precisely this aspect of overlapping definitions which is so confusing. When we see them all as the results of grace, however, as the consequences of God's blessing upon a congregation, then we are not surprised that they are closer to a continuous spectrum of God's blessing than to a series of isolated activities or functions. Rigid distinctions are neither profitable nor true to biblical usage.

Grace for quantitative growth of the church

For the fulfilment of quantitative goals the divinely provided means is the *charis* of God being actualized in parts of the spectrum of grace-gifts. Properly understood, the word *charismatic* cannot be reserved for certain enthusiastic fringe groups within both Protestant and Roman Catholic churches. Far from being peripheral or optional, we cannot anticipate on biblical grounds that the church will either grow quantitatively or be blessed qualitatively at all without the exercise of charismatic gifts. Thus it is quite irresponsible for us to polarize and to ignore discussion of the charismatic movement as being 'not for us'. We may deplore excesses, we may disagree with the understanding of *glōssa* and we may strongly dissent from the misleading usage of expressions like 'the baptism of the Spirit', but we cannot ignore the significance of *charismata* as a biblical category. It is not merely a question of recognizing that both in the Roman Catholic and Protestant churches there have been quickening and renewal of the church in association with this movement. It is more than just a pragmatic issue; it is a theological and doctrinal one. We have to face it because it is, as I am suggesting, the *charis of God*, this 'serving grace', which is *the only dynamic by which the church may grow and move to glorious consummation.*

This does not mean that we have to endorse all the peculiarities and idiosyncrasies of the so-called 'charismatic movement' which we may encounter. It is as foolish to insist on a blanket acceptance as it is wrong to make a blanket rejection. Everything must be carefully tested and proved from Scripture. It certainly seems clear from Scripture that the time will come when spiritual gifts are no longer required and will 'pass away' (1 Cor. 13). But that, it seems to me, is the time when that which is perfect is come and we see no longer 'in a glass darkly' but face to face with the returned Lord at his royal coming. Able and worthy expositors have done their best to prove that certain of the gifts have ceased. It seems difficult to maintain this biblically.

1. APOSTLES

It is interesting that it has been evangelical Anglicans in particular who have wanted to urge that there are no longer apostles. This understandably arises out of the Anglo-Catholic claim of apostolic authority and apostolic succession for bishops. Evangelicals have been rightly concerned to insist that apostolic doctrine and authority is now to be found in Scripture and that the original apostles by definition were 'men who have accompanied us all the time that the Lord Jesus went in and out among us, beginning with the baptism of John, until the day that he was taken up from us ... a witness with us of His resurrection' (Acts 1:21–22). I think that most of us would be prepared to accept that in this particular and unique sense the apostles no longer exist and that their authority is found today in Scripture.

Interestingly, expositors of other traditions[5] had no difficulty in recognizing a second category of apostles besides Paul, including Barnabas (Acts 14:14), Silas and Timothy (1 Thes. 2:6), Andronicus and Junia (Rom. 16:7; and Junia is regarded by Chrysostom as female!), Epaphroditus 'your apostle' (Phil. 2:25) and 'the apostles of the churches' (2 Cor. 8:23). It is rather comical to find some urging at one and the same time that the gift of apostleship has ceased and that there is a gift of being a missionary! The etymology of these two words from Greek and Latin respectively does suggest that the derived words should be regarded as parallel in meaning.

2. EVANGELISTS

In modern day parlance this would suggest the spiritual gift that is responsible for the multiplication of the number of Christians, the first category in our original list. However, this gift is mentioned only once (Eph. 4:11) and then among *domata* rather than *charismata*. Philip is referred to as 'the evangelist' (Acts 21:8) presumably to distinguish him from Philip the apostle, and Timothy is commanded to do the work of an evangelist (2 Tim. 4:5).

Why then is this spiritual gift not more frequently mentioned? It is possible to link the word 'evangelist' with the 'herald' or 'preacher' as, for example, on the two occasions when Paul says that he has been 'appointed a preacher and an apostle and a teacher' (2 Tim. 1:11; *cf.* 1 Tim. 2:7). The function of the herald is to proclaim the 'evangel' to the people who have not heard it before – which is exactly what an evangelist does. Another reason why this spiritual gift may not be mentioned more frequently is that it was necessarily exercised by the church-planting apostles (as a study of the verb 'to evangelize' in Acts makes clear).

[5] *E.g.* Vine's *Expository Dictionary of New Testament Words* (Oliphants, 1940).

The verb is used fifteen times in Acts and twenty times in Paul's epistles. Some significant uses refer to Philip the evangelist's ministry (Acts 8:5, 12, 25, 35, 40), to the ministry of Paul and Barnabas (Acts 13:82; 14:7, 21; 15:35) and subsequently to Paul's European mission (Acts 16:10; 17:18). This use of the verb supports the suggestion that this ministry is particularly one that an apostle must necessarily exercise, and is thus a classic example of overlap of gifts: apostles need to be evangelists.

We know, however, that this ministry was not confined to them, for not only was Philip the evangelist to evangelize, but there are at least two other references to evangelism by Christians in general (Acts 8:1, 4; 11:20). As we see from the use of the verb 'to evangelize' above, the two gifts immediately related to quantitative growth (not surprisingly) overlap with each other; although there are those who may evangelize who are not apostles, and apostles do many other things beside evangelizing.

The gift of an apostle is described as 'first' in 1 Corinthians 12:28 and is also at the head of two other lists (1 Cor. 12:29; Eph. 4:11). In every case it is mentioned as a personal office ('apostles') and not an aptitude ('apostleship') although that word does occur elsewhere. Certainly it would seem that *the primary function of apostles relates to the second quantitative category of church growth, that is, the multiplication of congregations.* The Acts of the Apostles provides us with a detailed and thrilling account of a church-planting ministry, particularly in Asia Minor on the first missionary journey and in Macedonia and Achaia on the second missionary journey. It seems self-evident that the chief work of apostles was starting new congregations in places where they had not previously existed. One notices that in writing to Corinth, for example, Paul is able to say 'I planted' (1 Cor. 3:6), 'I laid a foundation' (1 Cor. 3:10) and 'If to others I am not an apostle, at least I am to you; for you are the seal of my apostleship in the Lord' (1 Cor. 9:2).

When a pioneer missionary goes to a new tribe he finds

155

them with no Bible of their own. Initially he is their only source of apostolic doctrine so that, even in this secondary sense, he carries apostolic authority. It does not seem biblically necessary to deny the continuing existence of apostles in this secondary sense of pioneer church-planting missionaries. In missionary societies today we need this *charisma* more than any other. It is the 'first' of the gifts, and the planting of new congregations still needs to be done cross-culturally in many parts of the world. Although some kind of 'national church' may exist in nearly every country of the world the number of congregations may be pitifully few and pitifully small (Turkey or Iran), confined within certain ethnic groups (Indonesia), and castes (South India), as well as limited to certain geographical areas (Thailand). The need for a church-planting ministry remains. In some situations it may need to be done all over again as in Turkey where 'the seven churches of Asia Minor' no longer exist.

3. HEALING

I am deliberately raising various questions at this point, but it is an observable fact of church history that what we may for the sake of convenience refer to as 'miraculous gifts' (by which we particularly mean miracles and healing) seem to appear both in the New Testament and in the history of the missionary movement in situations of initial outreach, where God graciously provides visible and concrete evidence of his reality and power. These particular gifts may even have been seen as particularly (though not exclusively) being performed by apostles. Thus Paul could write, 'In no respect was I inferior to the most eminent apostles, even though I am a nobody. The signs of a true apostle were performed among you with all perseverance, by signs and wonders and miracles' (2 Cor. 12:11–12). This may well have been significant in the thinking of Luke in determining which incidents he should and should not include in the book of Acts. Thus *Peter* is involved in the healing of the man at the Beautiful

Gate of the temple (Acts 3:7) and the paralysed man Aeneas (Acts 9:33), while *Paul* healed the lame man at Lystra (Acts 14:10). Similarly there are only two recorded incidents of the raising of the dead in Acts, namely, when Peter raised the dead Tabitha at Joppa (Acts 9:40) and Paul appears to have raised Eutychus at Troas (Acts 20:10). This same emphasis seems to be made elsewhere, as, for example: 'After it was at the first spoken through the Lord, it was confirmed to us by those who *heard*, God also bearing witness with *them*, both by signs and wonders and by various miracles and by gifts of the Holy Spirit according to His own will' (Heb. 2:3–4).

In view of all the enthusiasm for spiritual gifts in recent years, and especially the services held for healing and the like, it is remarkable how relatively uncommon miracles of healing would seem to be in more developed countries today. It is also worth while noticing that even in the New Testament there is no specific reference in Acts to the healing of leprosy or restoration of sight to the blind, and only the two cases of raising the dead cited above. Just as the apostle Paul and the physician Luke worked side by side on the island of Malta, so in the last hundred and fifty years Christian doctors have worked alongside other missionaries, and just like Luke when he wrote his gospel, have themselves been evangelists. The commission of Jesus to the twelve and to the seventy to 'heal the sick' (Mt. 10:8; Lk. 10:9), while not given in the context of sending out to the nations (Mt. 28:19–20), is still seen to have an abiding relevance.

4. MIRACLES

The miracles performed in Acts do not seem to have included any 'nature miracles' like the plagues in Egypt or the Lord Jesus' stilling of the storm or feeding of the multitude (unless we regard Philip as miraculously levitated to Azotus in Acts 8:39–40). The New Testament miracles, however (distinguishing them from healings), appear to be of at least four kinds:

157

a. Miracles of judgment   The deaths of Ananias and Sapphira (Acts 5:5, 10) and the blindness of Elymas (Acts 13:11) are solemn examples.

b. Raising of the dead   Peter raised the dead Tabitha at Joppa (Acts 9:40) and Paul later appears to have raised Eutychus at Troas (Acts 20:10). These two apostles are recorded as having performed this miracle only once each in their lifetime.

c. Miracles of deliverance   On three occasions apostles were miraculously liberated from prison, twice by an angel of the Lord (Acts 5:19; 12:7) and once by an earthquake (Acts 16:26). Such miraculous deliverances from danger have been granted to missionaries in more recent times.[6]

d. Miracles of exorcism   Of the Seven, both Stephen and Philip performed great wonders and signs (Acts 6:8 and 8:6), some of them healings and some exorcisms (Acts 8:7). Later Paul and Barnabas performed signs and wonders in Iconium (Acts 14:3), and on his second missionary journey Paul cast out the evil spirit of clairvoyance from the slave girl (Acts 16:16–18).

Those of us who have lived abroad are familiar with situations where, in Chinese religion for example, individuals become possessed by an evil spirit or 'god', and in missionary situations the need for exorcism frequently occurs. Many of us, moving into a house where paper gods and wooden idols may still be on the walls, will have a brief service of burning and prayer for cleansing.

5. FAITH

This gift is mentioned only in the 1 Corinthians 12:4–11 list although it is referred to further in the following chapter: 'If I have all faith, so as to remove mountains, but do not have love, I am nothing' (1 Cor. 13:2). The reference to this gift in 1 Corinthians 12 is in the immediate context

[6] See, for example, *A Thousand Miles of Miracles in China* by Glover (CIM), for deliverances experienced in the Boxer Rising of 1900.

of the gift of healings and the effecting of miracles, and we may thus see a similar principle of overlap operating here, since both healing and miracles require a particular exercise of faith. In Matthew 17:20, the lack of faith to move mountains is the reason for the disciples' failure to cast demons out of a boy. In Mark 11:21–25, there is the further reference to a mountain-moving faith being exercised in prayer accompanied by the forgiveness of others. In Luke 17:3–6 mulberry-tree-moving faith is required to go on forgiving a brother who has sinned against you and asked for forgiveness seven times a day. Thus the biblical evidence for the meaning of this gift is scanty. However, we may certainly see that Elijah on Mount Carmel manifested a remarkable faith that the Lord would choose to vindicate himself and demonstrate his power in contrast to the weakness of the prophets of Baal (1 Ki. 18). Here was direct confrontation (it could scarcely be called dialogue!) with entrenched pagan religion.

In a New Testament pioneer situation it is surely not without significance that first it is said of Barnabas that 'he was a good man, and full of the Holy Spirit and *of faith*' and then immediately that 'considerable numbers were brought to the Lord' (Acts 11:24). There would seem to be some direct association in the mind of the writer between the fact that Barnabas was 'full of faith' and the fact that 'considerable numbers were brought to the Lord'.

Every new pioneer situation exposes the missionary to the fresh risk of faith. Will anything happen in this new town or village? However much he may have been used in other places, what will happen here? Every new missionary outreach brings the missionary fresh risk and the need for a renewed exercise of faith in God to show his power and to work. Although it is true that the missionary is often 'of little faith', this faith is something he must see as a *charisma*, that is, a fresh manifestation of God's grace in the new situation. This is also implied in the same passage about Barnabas who, 'when he had come and witnessed the *grace* of God, he rejoiced and began to encourage them all with resolute heart to remain true to the Lord' (Acts 11:23), reminding us, incidentally, that the gift of encouragement is also required by the pioneer apostle (although we shall deal with it in relation to qualitative growth).

6. SPEAKING IN LANGUAGES

Now I recognize that I am sticking my neck out here in espousing a viewpoint which may *at first sight* be uncharitably (and inaccurately) labelled as 'anti-charismatic'. I am open-minded on this subject and have no desire to throw any doubt upon the validity of the experience of respected friends and missionaries who see 'speaking in tongues' as something closely related to private prayer, through which their prayer life has been revolutionized and they themselves have been spiritually edified. It would be a serious misunderstanding, however, to think that I was being properly 'anti-charismatic' in saying this, for I am wanting to insist that *the 'gift of languages' and the closely related gift of 'interpretation' are essential to the cross-cultural missionary enterprise* and totally dependent upon the *charis* of God.

The gift of languages is referred to in all five of the Corinthian lists but, interestingly enough, in none of the others. How are we to understand this word *glōssa*? Does it mean that when we speak in 'tongues' we speak to God in prayer? That is certainly a possible understanding of it. Or could it mean that if you speak in your mother tongue, which may be incomprehensible to the rest of the congregation, you are certainly understood by God who understands all languages, but only edify yourself because nobody else understands what you are saying? Thus John Stott insists that, 'The noun *glōssa* has only two known meanings, namely the organ in the mouth and a language.'[7]

[7] J. R. W. Stott, *Baptism and Fullness* (IVP, 1975), p.112.

He goes on to suggest that a cardinal rule in biblical interpretation is that identical expressions have identical meaning, so that there is strong linguistic presumption that the word 'languages', referred to in Acts 2:4–11, has the same meaning also in 1 Corinthians: 12–14. After all, on the day of Pentecost Jerusalem was full of people speaking many languages; in a large cosmopolitan seaport city like Corinth there would have been many overseas visitors: 'Parthians and Medes and Elamites, and residents of Mesopotamia, Judea and Cappodocia, Pontus and Asia, Phrygia and Pamphylia, Egypt and the districts of Libya around Cyrene, . . . Cretans and Arabians . . . and visitors from Rome' (as in Acts 2:9–11). In such a multi-lingual port there must have been many occasions when someone wanted to speak in his own language words which would have been incomprehensible to the predominantly Greek-speaking congregation. Missionaries need the grace of God in order to communicate effectively in a different language.

No discussion today can overlook the fact that an essential component in a missionary's usefulness is his ability to speak one or more foreign languages. The time involved in learning a language and the restrictions stemming from inadequacies in speaking it will be a major factor during the first term of missionary service. In several countries people really need to learn two or more new languages! Every missionary society constantly wrestles with this problem of communication and a good deal of money is spent on providing language tuition.

Only the other day I came head on into collision with the problem of language. I was invited to preach to a Hokkien-speaking congregation in Taiwan: but the church had nobody available who reckoned that he could translate my English into Hokkien. The matter was finally settled by my preaching in Japanese and being translated directly into Hokkien.

If the problem exists in the modern world, it seems unrealistic to suppose that it never occurred in the ancient world. We seem to assume very readily that everybody in the Mediterranean world could speak and understand Greek, just as British tourists today seem to believe that everybody in the world can understand English if they speak it loudly enough! We know that Paul and Barnabas hit this problem at Lystra where the natives spoke the indigenous Lycaonian dialect (Acts 14:11–14). The fact that this problem did exist in Corinth is acknowledged when Paul says, '. . . if then I do not know the meaning of the language, I shall be to the one who speaks a barbarian and the one who speaks will be a barbarian to me' (1 Cor. 14:11). Just as many missionary travellers today, when invited to address a congregation, are faced with the question, 'Who will interpret?' such a problem *must* have occurred from time to time in the emerging congregations of the first century.

Anybody who has to preach in a recently acquired language recognizes how much he needs the 'grace-gift' from the Holy Spirit to speak effectively. It is an essential gift for taking the gospel to all nations. Human responsibility for applying oneself to language study is not removed, any more than is the responsibility for studying and preparing adequately before engaging in Christian teaching. But both teaching and speaking in languages, requiring as they do diligence in study and preparation, are seen properly as providing an opportunity for manifestation of the grace of God.

7. INTERPRETATION OF LANGUAGES

This gift is referred to in three lists and always, as might be expected, in association with the gift of languages.

In synagogue worship there was always an interpreter who, when the Scriptures were read in Ancient Hebrew, would translate them into contemporary Aramaic. Jews were familiar with the need for an interpreter. Interestingly, Aaron is described as Moses' interpreter and Papias refers to Mark as the 'interpreter' of Peter. The usage of the word strengthens the case for translating *glōssa* as (foreign) 'languages'. The word is also used in Luke 24:27 of Jesus when he 'explained . . . the things concerning Himself', and in John 1:38, 42; 9:7 and Acts 9:36 with the ordinary meaning of 'translated'.

Those of us who listen frequently to translated messages or who have to be interpreted ourselves are very clear that a gifted interpreter manifests the unction of the Spirit just as much or even more than the speaker whom he interprets. Just as with the gifts of teaching and of language, the need to study and to 'know our stuff' is not overridden, but the grace of God is manifest. This would seem to contradict the assertion that an interpreter of tongues need not understand the 'language' because he is speaking out the words which God gives him. The natural meaning of 'translate' in its general biblical usage seems to imply that the interpreter must have a direct understanding. Just as in preaching and teaching, however, where one is acutely conscious of the Spirit's help beyond one's own study, preparation or ability, both in the delivery and the choice of words, so also in interpretation the grace of the Lord may be manifested.

I hope it is emerging that while this discussion is naturally of interest to any student of the New Testament, a consideration of the gifts in an explicitly missionary context cannot help but throw further light on their proper understanding.

Grace for qualitative growth of the church

The understanding we have arrived at of *charismata* as manifestations of *charis* in the church, and the overlap between the different gifts, should cause us to avoid the error of specifically attaching some gifts to the quantitative growth of evangelism and church planting and others to the qualitative growth of church perfecting and edification. Indeed the list in Ephesians 4:11 suggests that apostles, prophets, evangelists and pastor/teachers alike have a responsibility for equipping the saints for the work of the ministry in order to build up the body of Christ;

and that apparently this will continue until the goal of a perfected church is reached (verse 13). While it could be argued that the ministry of Philip the evangelist in Samaria was incomplete without the complementary ministry of the apostles Peter and John (Acts 8:14), the ministry of the apostles Barnabas and Saul and Paul and Silas seems to have been used not only in pioneer evangelism and church planting, but in a continuing church-perfecting ministry among those same congregations. At the same time it can be argued that the ministry of prophets and teachers is required from the earliest period of a congregation's existence (Acts 13:1) so that the quantitative and qualitative aspects of church growth should not be regarded so much as consecutive as contemporaneous. The 'building up' begins with the very laying of the foundation and the very first course of bricks. Thus while it is convenient to distinguish between church-planting and church-perfecting ministries, these are all part of the continuing process, initiated by God employing human agents as his instruments by endowing them with his grace and enduing them with his power.

8. PROPHETS

Our understanding of this word is always fogged by the fact that the English usage, almost by definition, implies prediction of future events. While on only three occasions in the whole of the Acts of the Apostles is New Testament prophecy emphatically predictive,[8] various statements about prophecy are made on other occasions, where significantly the element of prediction is not even hinted at:

Acts 15:32   '. . . being prophets themselves, encouraged and strengthened the brethren with a lengthy message.'

1 Cor. 14:3   'One who prophesies speaks to men for

---

[8] Namely, Agabus' predictions of the famine and of Paul being bound (Acts 11:28; 21:10–11); and Paul's predictive prophecy about Jews and Gentiles (Acts 28:25–28).

edification and exhortation and consolation.'

1 Cor. 14:31 'You can all prophesy one by one, so that all may learn and all may be exhorted.'

It can be seen at once that here the gift of prophecy overlaps with the gift of encouragement and also (1 Cor. 14:31) with teaching('all may learn'), a further typical overlapping between the gifts of grace.

These verses also remind us of another complication, ably explained by Earle Ellis: 'In several passages in Acts, the phenomenon of prophecy is ascribed to Christian disciples generally . . . Alongside these texts is the equally significant fact that Luke restricts the term or title *prophētēs*, as it is used of his contemporaries, to a select number of "leading men" (*cf.* Acts 15:22) who exercise considerable influence in the Christian community.[9]

In very similar vein F. F. Bruce, commenting on I Corinthians 14:31, says that 'The ability to prophesy, at least on occasion, is open to most, indeed to all, members of the church, although only a few may exercise it at any one meeting, speaking one by one, so that all may learn and all be encouraged. In 11:4f., prophesying appears to be as common an exercise as praying and that on the part of men and women alike . . .'[10]

One of the other problems about the English word 'prophet' as opposed to the actual biblical usage of *prophētēs* is that it suggests not only that which is uniformly predictive, but also that which is uniquely authoritative. In view of the fact that 'you can all prophesy one by one', this concept of authority needs considerable modification. Even the Roman Catholic doctrine of infallibility allows it only to one man at a time when he speaks *ex cathedra*

[9] E. Ellis, 'The Role of a Christian Prophet in Acts', in W. W. Gasque and R. P. Martin (eds.), *Apostolic History and the Gospel* (*Festschrift* for F. F. Bruce: Paternoster Press, 1970), p.55.

[10] F. F. Bruce, *1 and 2 Corinthians* (*New Century Bible*, Oliphants, 1971), p.134.

(*i.e.* in council and consultation with the doctors of the church). As Protestants, no-one ought to substitute a new doctrine of the infallibility of every believer, man or woman, who happens to prophesy! We notice accordingly that provision is made for critical discernment. Thus in 1 Corinthians 14, when a church member prophesies the rest should 'judge' or 'weigh' what has been said, and while prophesyings are not to be despised they are to be tested carefully (1 Thes. 5:20–21). Equally clearly, however, there are some like Silas and the five at Antioch (who included Paul and Barnabas) who particularly carry the title of prophet or indeed prophetess (Acts 21:9).[11]

We should notice that it is clearly one of the gifts which helps in perfecting the saints and making the church aware of how the word of God is relevant to their present situation in the world.

Because of the overlap already indicated between 'prophets' and 'teachers' and the fact that one of the results of prophesying is that 'all may learn', we should be most cautious about the kind of criticism which negates some explanations of 'prophecy' as 'little more than teaching'. One can neither teach nor prophesy without the help of the Holy Spirit. Both alike are the results of God's grace, and there is considerable overlap between the two gifts. 'If any man speak, let him speak as the oracles of God' (1 Pet. 4:11, AV), and in any one oracle there may well be a mixture of elements which are distinctly prophetic and others which are distinctly didactic. But both alike should be seen as a word from God and both need the Spirit of God for their inspiration. It should be noticed that Old Testament prophets did study Scripture as a basis for their pronouncements: Daniel, for example, studied Jeremiah (Dn. 9:2,24).

Over and over again in newly formed congregations crises occur where a powerful application of relevant scriptural passages to the immediate problems seems

[11] For a full treatment Earle Ellis (*art. cit.*) is most helpful.

emphatically prophetic in this sense. Longer-established churches need also the prophetic voice to shake them awake to their peril and need for repentance, as in John's ministry to the seven churches (Rev. 2–4).

9. TEACHERS

The gift of teaching is listed third (Rom. 12:7), overlapping on the one hand with prophets (Acts 13:1) and on the other with pastors (Eph. 4:11). Teaching is the primary means of edifying the church and building up the body. The word group comprising *didaskō* (94 times), *didaskalos* (58 times), *didaskalia* (21 times), and *didache* (29 times) is one found extremely frequently throughout the New Testament. We should not forget associated words like *mathēteuō* (to teach, to make a disciple) *noutheteō* (to admonish) and *nouthesia* (admonition) and others.

We should notice that the great commission commits us to two significant forms of teaching. We are to make disciples (*mathēteuō*), in other words to teach with a view to commitment, and we are to 'teach them to obey everything which Christ commanded us', with a view to behavioural change. We are thus to get rid of the mental image of merely imparting information to people long enough to enable them to pass examinations. It is teaching in a fully biblical sense which is one of the ways by which the Holy Spirit changes and transforms the congregation from one degree of glory to another. If we are to have an effective ministry in the church, then we must pray that God will manifest his grace in giving *teachers* to his church in order to perfect his saints and bring us to the unity of the faith and of the knowledge of his Son.

10. PASTORS

The single reference in Ephesians 4:11 to a pastor/ shepherd as a spiritual gift (*domata*) is coupled with the gift of teacher, where the absence of the article suggests that 'pastors/teachers' are a single group. Most of the biblical references to this word (*poimēn*) are either to literal shepherds or to Jesus himself as the Good Shepherd. However, the use of the *verb* (*poimainō*) makes shepherding the responsibility of the *apostle* Peter (Jn. 21:16) and Peter himself teaches *elders* to shepherd the flock (1 Pet. 5:2), while Paul similarly instructs the Ephesian elders (Acts 20:28). We may therefore explain the solitary reference to the pastoral gift in combination with the gift of teaching as being a general function of the local church elder. The shepherding gift may be partly verbal in terms of individual teaching and admonition, but begins to move into the more administrative group of words (see *Administrations* below).

The weakness of nominal chuches often arises because the ministers are failing to apply themselves to the pastoral task, like the faithless shepherds of Ezekiel 34:4: 'Those who are sick you have not strengthened, the diseased you have not healed, the broken you have not bound up, the scattered you have not brought back, nor have you sought for the lost; but with force and severity you have dominated them.' While our ministerial training remains predominantly a matter of stuffing people with academic content rather than of using that content to shepherd the flock, this neglect of pastoral functions explains the 'wood, hay and stubble' quality of many churches.

11. HE WHO ENCOURAGES

The gift mentioned specifically as such in Romans 12:8 was so much a manifestation of grace in the life of one of the apostles that he was even nicknamed after it (Acts 4:36, 'son of encouragement'). The verb, however, is an extremely common one in relation both to the ministry of church-planting apostles and more generally to the need to encourage Christians to stand firm in the face of discouragement, suffering and persecution.[12] As we have seen, it relates very closely with one of the results of the

[12] It is used 23 times in Acts and 49 times in the Pauline epistles.

168

ministry of prophecy. Paul tells Timothy to give attention to the exhortation (1 Tim. 4:13, *lē paraklēsei*) where the definite article suggested that, like *the* reading, *the* exhortation was an accepted and anticipated part of public worship. It is used in this sense in the synagogue at Pisidian Antioch when 'after the reading of the law and the prophets the synagogue officials sent to them, saying "Brethren, if you have any word of exhortation for the people, say it"' (Acts 13:15). Paul's injunction to Timothy to give attention to (*proseche*; 1 Tim. 4:13) would appear to imply previous private preparation before public ministry. This particular use of 'encouragement' seems to approach very closely to what today we call expository preaching.

12. LEADERSHIP

The idea of leadership has already been included in the idea of the pastoral gift, where in the Middle East the shepherd leads his flock; but it is also implied by a number of other words.

a. Administrations (kubernēsis) is derived from the word *kubernetes*, used in the New Testament for a ship's captain (Rev. 18:17) or steersman (Acts 27:11, even if that one did land them up on the rocks!). Just as the helmsman steers or pilots the ship, so those with gifts of 'direction' should guide the progress of a congregation. The same word is used in the LXX of 'counsellors' (Pr. 1:5; 11:14; 24:6) which Kittel suggests would be best translated by 'clever direction'.[13] Thus as Captain Hornblower is always thinking ahead and directing the course of his ship in the face of battle and many other hazards, so those with the Christian gifts of leadership need the grace of God in order to steer the congregation.

b. He who leads (proistamenoi) is used in Romans 12:8 of the gift of presiding and is also referred to in 1 Thessalonians 5:12. The church needs not only gifted teachers

[13] G. Kittel (ed.), *Theological Dictionary of the New Testament* (Eerdmans).

but gifted chairmen who may help a divided congregation to come to a common mind (*e.g.* Acts 15:13, James at the Council of Jerusalem).

c. Leaders (hegoumenoi) occurs three times in Hebrews 13 while Silas and Judas Barsabbas are described as leading men among the brethren (Acts 15:22). It is perhaps worthy of comment that in times past, with the exception of the squire, the parson was the only literate member of the congregation. He was expected to exercise many varied gifts. This traditional pattern has produced today the omnicompetent vicar or non-conformist minister. The assumption seems to be that one man will possess the whole range of spiritual gifts. But not all good teachers are good leaders, and not all good leaders are good teachers.

The *qualitative* growth of the church will be achieved only when we move away from the one-man-band ministry to a recovery of an every-man-and-woman ministry within the congregation. If the congregation goes to the church building expecting that one man is going to fulfil all of these functions, then we have something which is qualitatively less developed and less satisfying than the situation where the whole church comes together expecting each member to exercise his or her own distinctive functions to the upbuilding of the whole body.

13. GIFTS OF SERVICE

The apostle Peter, speaking of the gift (*charisma*) which each has received (1 Pet. 4:10–11), distinguishes between 'whoever speaks' and 'whoever serves' while service (*diakonia*) is referred to among the gifts listed in Romans 12:6–8. With this gift we may associate the 'he who gives' and 'he who shows mercy' of the same passage and the 'helps' (*antilēmpsis*) of 1 Corinthians 12:28. This last is a rare word, not used elsewhere in canonical Scripture (although the verbal form is found in Acts 20:35, '. . . you must *help* the weak', as well as in Lk. 1:54). According to Bittlinger this is used too (in a recently discovered papyrus) as a technical word in the field of banking and refers to the administration of money.[14] If this is so, it suggests the person who has the responsibility of helping the poor by almsgiving and would be the closest word to 'treasurer' in our current vocabulary. We should not overlook the allusion, 'If I turn all my property into morsels of food to feed the poor' (1 Cor. 13:3). *There is definitely a social aspect to building up the congregation.* It is anticipated that it will make some impact upon the community at large by following the commands of its master who 'preached the gospel to the poor'.

It is important to insist that such practical helps are also *charismata* and that the work or organizers, treasurers, typists, house parents, hostesses, *etc.*, is thoroughly biblical and requires the grace of the Holy Spirit just as much as speaking gifts. Paul compares the importance of such quiet and discreet members with the human organs of reproduction, modestly concealed, but at least as important as the organs of hearing and seeing (1 Cor. 12:22–26).

Conclusions

The so-called 'charismatic renewal', then, should surely not be regarded merely as some kind of strange new teaching, but welcomed as leading us to a fresh understanding of the means whereby the body of the church is to be edified and to move towards its goals. We should not allow some of its more socially embarrassing cultural *mores* like hand-clapping, arm-raising and the repetition of choruses to cause us to overlook its significance both for worship and for the mobilization of the whole congregation.

In a former generation, missionary pioneers like Paget Wilkes of Japan urged the necessity of an anointing with power by the Holy Spirit for effective missionary work. Today we may not find it acceptable to apply directly to ourselves the words of the Lord Jesus to the apostles

[14] Arnold Bittlinger, *Gifts and Graces* (Hodder, 1973).

before Pentecost, when he commanded them to tarry in Jerusalem and to wait for what the Father had promised: 'You shall receive power when the Holy Spirit has come upon you; and you shall be My witnesses both in Jerusalem, and in all Judea and Samaria, and even to the remotest part of the earth' (Acts 1:8). But it was this Pentecostal experience which resulted in the outpouring of grace and power upon the Jerusalem church. While we may properly insist that Pentecost was a unique and unrepeatable historical experience, the whole church none the less needs to enter existentially into an enjoyment of that same experience of grace and power for our own ministry, whether at home or overseas. The proper place to finish this chapter is on our knees declaring: 'Lord, without you I can do nothing: fill me with your grace and power that I may bear much lasting fruit for your glory. Amen.'

Material for study

Howard A. Snyder, 'The Church as God's Agent in Evangelism', *LTEHHV*, p.327.

J. R. W. Stott, *Baptism and Fullness* (IVP, 1975).

M. C. Griffiths, *Cinderella's Betrothal Gifts* (OMF, 1978)

David C. K. Watson, *I Believe in the Church* (Hodder, 1978).

Questions for discussion

1. Mission is the mission of God. He guarantees its final success. But how far does he limit himself to work through men in the church? Does 1 Corinthians 3 not imply that man is allowed to build shoddily or even to demolish the church? He gives grace to wise master builders, and 'grace and power' to his people. Is the rediscovery of the many-gifted local church 'body' therefore significant?

2. Do you find a place for apostles in some secondary sense in current missionary work?

3. Discuss the problem of the overlap of gifts, especially apostle, prophet, teacher, evangelist and encourager.

4. If *charismata* are given sovereignly by the Lord (1 Cor. 12:11, 18) what is our human responsibility in response to God's *charis*?

6 The multi-racial dream of completed mission and glorified church

The church, according to Moltmann, 'is like an arrow sent out into the world to point to the future'.[1] We live in a world where everybody is interested in the future. Whether in political or scientific terms everybody wants a more beautiful future; and some look for it in a socialist utopia, a future classless, marxist society. The biblical idea of the kingdom of God has been replaced by the goal of a perfect earthly society. And so immortality is collective, not personal; the survival of the state rather than the individual. Totalitarian states in the last few decades have eliminated thousands of unwanted human beings in the interests of their new social order. Many people share this 1984 cynicism about a future 'Animal Farm' of human animals where party members are more equal than others. Lesslie Newbigin criticises another equally unacceptable alternative:

> The meaning of human life is to be found in the spiritual history of the individual. The destiny of the individual soul becomes the ultimate goal of the whole story; and the whole drama of human history, of politics, of war, of revolution, the whole story of world history, has no meaning and no ending. It is not a drama, it is the only thing which can quite properly be called a non-stop revue providing the setting for a series

[1] Jürgen Moltmann, *Theology of Hope* (ET, SCM Press, 1967).

of solo items after which each of the players goes off and receives his bouquet privately in the wings ... The whole meaning of life is exhausted in the quest of personal immortality.[2]

In the developed countries, in spite of their material progress, there remains an insatiable longing for a better and more ideal world and an escape through literature and television into utopian fantasies of Narnia, Hobbits, *Watership Down*, where all brave rabbits are equal, or a *Logan's Run* to Sanctuary which offers escape from death to teenagers and adults alike. Space rockets engage in *Star Wars*. Every 'with-it' preacher needs to be literate in the present day mythology of star trekking with Kirk and Spock, *Blake's Seven* and the current incarnation of *Dr Who*. They are all symptomatic of man's heart-cry for something else. Is there no new adventurous community with a beautiful lifestyle fulfilling man's true destiny in the future? Does the gospel have nothing to say? If you leave out what the Bible says about *the future* – the promises, most of the parables, reference to the kingdom, and the coming of the Son of man – you will find you have little gospel left.

> From first to last, and not merely in the epilogue, Christianity is eschatology, is hope, forward looking and forward moving, and therefore also revolutionizing and transforming the present. The eschatological is not one element *of* Christianity, but it is the medium of Christian faith as such, the key in which everything in it is set, the glow that suffuses everything here in the dawn of an expected new day. For Christian faith lives from the raising of the crucified Christ, and strains after the promises of the universal future of Christ. Eschatology is the passionate suffering and passionate longing kindled by the Messiah. Hence eschatology cannot really be only a part of Christian doctrine. Rather, the eschatological outlook is char-

[2] L. Newbigin, *A Faith for this one World?* (SCM Press, 1961), p.98.

acteristic of all Christian proclamation, of every Christian existence and of the whole church.[3]

The church has so often lost its way. Under Constantine it became a *cultus publicus*, merely providing the establishment with its religious resources; in post-Christian Europe a *cultus privatus*, degenerating into individualistic piety, the escape of the Christian individual from the hostile world around him. It merely exists in the present with an endless round of program-orientated activities, like Pooh and Piglet following their own footprints round and round the tree! Mission on the other hand cannot so easily avoid asking questions. Saving souls from what and for what? Planting churches of what quality? When is our work finished? Any viable theology of church and mission is bound to ask the ultimate eschatological questions. *You cannot have a program for perfected church and completed mission without thinking in eschatological terms.*

Let me try and clarify the question to which we must find an answer. We anticipate ultimately a perfected church, without spot or wrinkle (Eph. 5:27); a completed mission with the gospel preached ,to all nations (Mt. 24:14); a visible and victorious Lord bringing everything to final consummation with his *parousia*, his great royal visit, and handing over the kingdom to his Father (1 Cor. 15:24). What are the intermediate stages by which we move from where the church is at this moment to where it will be then at the *parousia*? In the opening chapter we looked at some of the immediate goals of church and mission, but in the final chapter I want to point you to the biblical goals of consummation when we all 'attain to the unity of the faith, and of the knowledge of the Son of God, to a mature man, to the measure of the stature which belongs to the fullness of Christ' (Eph. 4:13).

How soon do you expect this to happen? Are you cyn-

[3] Moltmann, *op. cit.*, p.16.

ical about the church and its chances? Although you may feel it disloyal to verbalize it, are you subconsciously defeatist? Do you expect to see a significant advance of the church towards its goal in your lifetime? Is it possible to sketch out what may be anticipated in the next century of church history? Or does that sound quite crazy? Paul described how a newly planted church turned to God to *'wait for his Son from heaven'* (1 Thes. 1:9–10). Christians are meant to have this sense of anticipation; this waiting with craning neck for Christ's momentous 'royal visit'. Do Christians who pray daily 'Your kingdom come' expect this prayer to be answered? And what will it be like when it happens? The 'Sleeping Beauty' knows that 'Some day my prince will come' – he whom Peter calls 'the prince of life' (Acts 3:15).

The royal visit (*'the glorious appearing'*, Tit. 2:13)

The word *parousia* carries 'a quasi-technical force from Ptolemaic times onwards, to denote the "visit" of a king, emperor or other person in authority.'[4] It is this word, associated in everyday speech with a royal visit (also used in the imperial cult) that Paul uses of the anticipated coming of Christ. It is the word used by Jesus himself of the 'coming of the Son of Man' (Mt. 24:3, 27, 37, 39). Paul uses it on seven occasions in reference to the coming of Christ.[5] It is worth noticing that familiar expressions like 'heralding the gospel of the kingdom' (Mt. 4:23) contain two other common words associated with this deliberate use of the language of royalty. Other less common ideas also appear; the word for the reception committee which went out to greet a ruler on a *parousia* is *apantēsis*, alluded to in 1 Thessalonians 4:17 where the saints who

---

[4] J. H. Moulton and G. Milligan, *Vocabulary of the Greek Testament* (Hodder, 1930).

[5] 1 Cor. 15:23; and six times in the Thessalonian letters (1 Thes. 2:19; 3:13; 4:15; 5:23; 2 Thes. 2:1, 8). It is also used with the same royal meaning twice in James (5:7–8), three times in 2 Peter (1:16; 3:4, 12) and also in 1 John (2:28).

176

are at that time alive, Paul writes, will be caught up '*to meet* the Lord in the air'. Another rather pleasing reference is the one where Paul likens the Thessalonian congregation to a 'crown . . . in the presence of our Lord Jesus at his royal coming' (1 Thes. 2:19 and Phil. 4:1). Thus, according to Kittel, 'customary honours on the *parousia* of a ruler included tribute, improvement of streets, golden wreaths' while Moulton and Milligan cite a papyrus in which contributions were requested for a 'crown' to be presented to a king on his arrival.[6] The figure is a striking one: the missionary church planter and the faithful minister of the gospel go forth to meet the King of kings at his royal coming and lay at his feet the beautiful, purified, sparkling crown of the sanctified congregation. It is to this end that we study theology in the first place: in order to to be prepared for such a church-planting and church-perfecting ministry.

The believer's refashioned body ('*like his glorious body*', Phil. 3:21)

In the letter to the Thessalonians Paul describes how those saints who are still alive will be reunited with those who have fallen asleep in Jesus, whom the coming King will bring with him (1 Thes. 4:13–18). The language of the other Macedonian epistle also speaks of our citizenship in heaven from which we wait for Jesus Christ, describing him by borrowing the language of the imperial cult and contrasting the Roman emperor with the greater than Caesar who is coming, by calling him both *sōtēr* and *kurios*. He then goes on to say that he will transform (*metaschēmatisei*) the body of our humiliation to become like (*summorphon*) his glorious body (Phil. 3:20–21). There would seem to be a deliberate allusion here to the language of the confessional hymn (Phil. 2:6–11) when he who was in the form (*morphē*) of God from the beginning took the form of a servant and was found in fashion

---

[6] Kittel, *op. cit.*; Moulton and Milligan, *op. cit.*

(*schēmati*) as a man. As some modern writers clearly bring out,[7] biblical eschatology is the direct product of biblical Christology and this is an important theme in Moltmann's *Theology of Hope*. The incarnation of the pre-incarnate Christ as man and his consequent glorification to the right hand of God implies also the resurrection and glorification of redeemed men and women.

Thus, when in the Apostles' Creed we declare our faith in 'the forgiveness of sins, the resurrection of the body', we are recognizing that the resurrection of the bodies of believers results directly from a faith in the bodily resurrection of Jesus from the dead as 'the first fruits of those who are asleep' (1 Cor. 15:20). It is 'Christ the first fruits, and after that those who are Christ's at his *parousia*' (1 Cor. 15:23). We notice also that the resurrection of those who have fallen asleep is directly related to believing in Jesus' resurrection. Our resurrection is conditional upon our believing in his: 'For *if* we believe that Jesus died and rose again, even so God will bring with Him those who have fallen asleep in Jesus' (1 Thes. 4:14). A 'John Brown's body' doctrine of the resurrection, of a Jesus whose body lies mouldering in the grave while the spirit of the eternal Jesus goes marching on, will not do justice either to the Bible or to the historic formulations of the Christian faith found in the creeds.

Whether one is living in Buddhist, Islamic, Confucian or Taoist societies the underlying animism always seems to outcrop in the despair of death and the fatalism of funerals. It is precisely here that biblical Christianity is 'authoritative good news' to those who grieve with no hope (1 Thes. 4:13). It is a marvellous doctrine of encouragement for missionaries to preach to those whose living bodies are rotted away and deformed by leprosy. All modern cures and treatment which missionary medicine performs are at the most an amelioration and a postponement

[7] *E.g.* 'The Christological basis of Christian hope', in G. B. Caird *et al.*, *The Christian Hope* (SPCK, 1970).

178

of the coming of bodily death and putrefaction. The gospel is not good news at all unless it is firmly eschatological in a full biblical sense.

The transformation of the church (*'a glorious church'*, Eph. 5:27)

The New Testament speaks not only of a salvation for individuals and the expectation that our bodies will become like *'his glorious body'* but also of a *'glorious church'* having no spot or wrinkle(Eph. 5:27). There is great personal comfort in knowing that our aging and failing human bodies are to be refashioned. In all our criticism of the institutional churches with all their many spots and wrinkles, it is a great corporate encouragement to know that ultimately there is also a corporate salvation for the human community. For too long pietistic Protestantism has taught an individualistic salvation predominantly concerned with posthumous benefits in heaven. As we have seen above, this is an important part of the gospel, but it is not the whole of the gospel. We may also rejoice in the anticipation of a perfected and glorified community, the church of the living God (1 Tim. 3:15). Thus we are all to pray that God may establish our hearts 'unblamable in holiness before our God and Father at the royal coming of our Lord Jesus with all his saints' (1 Thes. 3:13); and we can anticipate that 'the God of peace Himself (will) sanctify the congregation entirely and . . . your spirit and soul and body be preserved complete without blame at the coming of our Lord Jesus Christ' (1 Thes. 5:23). The use of words like *epiteleō* (Phil. 1:6), *epistērizō* and *katartizō* are all constant reminders of God's determination to build his church perfectly. The same expectation is found in Hebrews: '. . . encouraging one another; and all the more, as you see the day drawing near' (Heb. 10:25); and in Peter: '. . . what sort of people ought you to be in holy conduct and godliness, looking for and hastening the *parousia* of the day of God . . .' (2 Pet. 3:11–12). This quotation leads us neatly into the next section, as it continues,

179

'But according to His promise we are looking for new heavens and a new earth, in which righteousness dwells' (2 Pet. 3:13).

The renewal of the whole creation (*'the glorious liberty of the sons of God'*, Rom. 8:21)

Salvation is not only individual and corporate, but also cosmic. It is clear that the New Testament 'speaks of the earnest anticipation, the neck-craning expectancy, of the whole splendid theatre of the universe and of all the manifold sub-human life within it as eagerly awaiting the revelation of the sons of God'.[8] There is a very real danger that we shall be so other-worldly with our eyes turned to heaven that we do not have a fully biblical doctrine of this present creation. We expect some continuity between our present personalities and our future glorious bodies and between the church militant on earth and the church triumphant in heaven. Ought we not equally, then, to expect some similar continuity between this creation and the *new* heavens and the *new* earth? Caird is most interesting on this:

> Too often evangelical Christianity has treated the souls of men as brands plucked from the burning and the world in general as a grim vale of soul-making. It has been content to see the splendour of the created universe, together with all brilliant achievements of human labour, skill and thought, as nothing more than the expendable backdrop for the drama of redemption. One of the reasons why men of our generation have turned against conventional Christianity is that they think it involves writing off the solid joys of this present life for the doubtful acquisition of some less substantial treasure.[9]

The Bible (in Rom. 8:19–21) teaches that the sub-

[8] C. E. B. Cranfield, 'Some observations on Romans 8:19–21' from R. Banks (ed.), *Reconciliation and Hope*: New Testament Essays on Atonement and Eschatology Presented to Leon Morris on his 60th Birthday (Paternoster Press, 1974), p.226.

[9] G. C. Caird, *op. cit.*, p.21.

human creation has been subjected to the frustration of not being able properly to fulfil the purpose of its existence. It has suffered the ineffectiveness of that which fails to attain its goal. Cranfield is superb on this:

> The whole magnificent theatre of the universe, together with all its splendid properties and all the varied chorus of sub-human life, created for God's glory, is cheated of its true fulfilment so long as man, the chief actor in the great drama of God's praise, fails to contribute his rational part. The Jungfrau and the Matterhorn and the planet Venus and all living things too, man alone excepted, do indeed glorify God in their own ways; but, since their praise is destined to be not a collection of independent offerings but part of a magnificent whole, the united praise of the whole creation, they are prevented from being fully that which they were created to be, so long as man's part is missing, just as all the other players in a concerto would be frustrated of their purpose if the soloist were to fail to play his part.[10]

Our theology then must have room for *apokatastasis* ('. . . whom heaven must receive until the period of restoration of all things about which God spoke by the mouth of his holy prophets from ancient time', Acts 3:21).[11] It must have room for *palingenesia* when Jesus said to them, 'Truly I say to you, that you have followed Me, in the regeneration when the Son of Man will sit on His glorious throne, you also shall sit upon twelve thrones, judging the twelve tribes of Israel' (Mt. 19:28). The idea of *palingenesia* was used by the Stoics for that restoration of nature every spring when everything is fresh, bursting with new life, and yet not totally discontinuous with what precedes it, but rather the anticipated fulfilment of it. This concept of the spring is used by Albrecht Bengel (1687–1752) when

[10] C. E. B. Cranfield, *op. cit.*, p.227.
[11] Notice, incidentally, that Jesus is in heaven until the restoration takes place – a very difficult verse for millennialists to include in their system.

he writes that 'the approach of better times for Christianity may be compared to the gradual peep of verdure through the dissolving snow, with here and there a green patch more or less conspicuous. The large wintry covering spread over all the nations, and which *we* are waiting to see dissolved, consists of Mohammedism, Popery and Infidelity. These are alike, as amounting to one and the same usurpation over immortal souls.'[12]

The theological vindication for this expectation is suggested by Caird when he writes,

> At first reading we may receive the impression that while the millennium is the vindication of God's purposes within history, the new heaven and earth are discontinuous with the old one which has been rolled up like a scroll. But this is to take the imagery too pedantically. For we are told that into the New Jerusalem shall be brought the wealth and splendour of the nations, though nothing unclean may enter it (Rev. 21:26–7). Not only are the gates of the city open on all sides to receive the numberless company of its citizens, everything of real worth in the old heaven and earth, including the achievements of man's inventive, artistic and intellectual prowess, will find a place in the eternal order.[13]

This is surely the 'kingdom of God' to which the church is on its way, and which the victorious Jesus will deliver up to his Father at his *royal coming* at the *end* (1 Cor. 15:23–24).

Having laid the groundwork of Christian expectation of what is to happen with the royal coming of the King, we are now in a position to return to our question about the intermediate stages on the way to completed mission and perfected church. Paul speaks of these two categories when he talks both of the 'progress of the gospel' (Phil. 1:12) and 'your progress' (Phil. 1:25; *i.e*, of the Phi-

---

[12] J. C. F. Burk, *Memoir of the Life and Writings of John Albrecht Bengel*, translated by R. F. Walker, 1837, p.316.
[13] Caird, *op. cit.*, p.24.

lippian congregation). Paul saw his apostolic labouring and suffering as directed towards these two great goals. It is this sense of commitment, progress and advance which rings through Paul's writings. They carry the inevitable challenge: *are we committed to the progress of his gospel in the world and the progress of his glory in the church?*

Evangelicals have tended to ignore this biblical truth because theological liberalism's expectation of the kingdom of God on earth was little more than pagan hopefulness, veneered with Christianity, based on a false belief in the inevitable moral and social progress of humanity as a whole.

The preaching of the gospel of the kingdom to all nations

Scripture is very clear in saying 'the gospel must first be preached to all the nations' (Mk. 13:10) and 'this gospel of the kingdom shall be preached in the whole world for a witness to all the nations, and then the end shall come' (Mt. 24:14). There is a task of world-wide evangelization to be completed before the *parousia* takes place. 'The proclamation of the gospel to all nations itself becomes a 'sign' of the end, an integral element in the eschatological divine plan of salvation.'[14]

Lesslie Newbigin expresses it in his characteristically refreshing way by saying that 'the church is in motion . . . It is a pilgrim people on its way to the promised land. The end to which it moves is the full realization of the reign of God.' Thus the church is the instrument and the first fruit of the kingdom. It has always been a body *sent*; it not only has a mission, 'it is a mission, a continuation of God's mission'. The present is given to us for the gospel of the kingdom to be made known and for men to repent and believe. 'Therefore there is urgency. There is not an

[14] Oscar Cullmann, 'Eschatology and Missions in the New Testament', in G. H. Anderson (ed.), *The Theology of the Christian Mission* (SCM Press, 1961), p.46.

infinity of time before us.' Mission has often been seen within the general evolutionary idea of development, the gradual permeation of the world by Christianity. But the New Testament seems to have a different perspective: 'The end is near. The gospel must be preached to every creature. There must be no tarrying for those who will not hear. The messengers must push on as soon as they can to the ends of the earth. That is the task committed to us.'[15]

But then we begin to ask the question: has the gospel not yet been preached to all nations? We would certainly seem to be approaching that point. Some of the few totally closed countries have become open in recent years (for example Nepal and Bhutan now have a few medical missionaries). Some time ago it was said that Mauritania in Africa and the Mongolian Republic were the only two countries in the world without any Christians at all. Certainly we are able to say that there are now Christians in nearly every country in the world, although we have to add at once that in some their numbers are miserably few. Have most Arabs had the chance to hear the gospel? And have they heard it proclaimed in a way that makes it possible for them to understand? And even if they do understand, are they genuinely free to respond?

In an interesting book[16] Iain Murray gives a fascinating account of Puritan and early missionary expectations of an unprecedented time of spiritual blessing before the Lord's return when 'the Gospel would triumph across the entire globe'. This expectation was associated with the anticipation of the turning of Israel to Jesus Christ. Murray quotes Charles Simeon responding to the question 'Six millions of Jews and six hundred millions of Gentiles – which is the most important?' with the scribbled reply, 'If the conversion of the six is to be life from the dead to

---

[15] L. Newbigin, *A Faith for this one World?* (SCM Press, 1961), p.103.
[16] I. Murray, *The Puritan Hope* (Banner of Truth, 1971).

the six hundred, what then?'[17] Murray also expounds Romans 11, particularly 'Now if the fall of them be the riches of the world, and the diminishing of them the riches of the Gentiles; how much more their fullness? . . . For if the casting away of them be the reconciling of the world what shall the receiving of them be, but life from the dead?' (Rom. 11:12, 15, AV).

He goes on to show most convincingly that this expectation was eclipsed as a result of the teaching of Henry Irvine who in turn influenced J. N. Darby and subsequently C. I. Scofield. The prevailing doctrine then became a thorough pessimism about the world and such an expectation of the imminent return of Christ that it 'totally forbids all working for earthly objects distant in time'.[18] This unfortunate result of dispensational pre-millennialist teaching was further accentuated by reaction against the 'social gospel' of liberal theology as described earlier. 'The wonder of God's saving works ought therefore to make Christians slow to believe that only doom and catastrophe must await the vast population of this evil earth.'[19] It is this pessimistic attitude which refuses to believe that 'the end is not yet' (Mt. 24:6) which C. H. Spurgeon opposed when he wrote,

> David was not a believer in the theory that the world will grow worse and worse, and that the dispensation will wind up with general darkness, and idolatry. Earth's sun is to go down amid ten-fold night if some of our prophetic brethren are to be believed. Not so do we expect, but we look for a day when the dwellers in all lands shall learn righteousness, shall trust in the Saviour, shall worship Thee alone, O God, 'and shall glorify Thy Name'. The modern notion has greatly damped the zeal of the Church for Missions, and the sooner it is shown to be unscriptural the better for the cause of God.

[17] I. Murray, *op. cit.*, p.155.
[18] *Ibid.*, p.203.
[19] *Ibid.*, p.xx.

It neither consorts with prophecy, honours God, nor inspires the Church with ardour. Far hence be it driven.[20]

While we may rejoice that the gospel has made such progress we all hesitate to say that it has been preached to all nations. When one meets the hearty individual who says: 'Isn't it wonderful that Christ may return tomorrow', I personally do not find it easy to make an enthusiastic response. My heart cries out for those who have not yet had the opportunity to hear and respond.

But let us come back to this matter of time scale for a moment. In Ruth Rouse's most interesting article, 'William Carey's Pleasing Dream',[21] she reminds us of the proposal made by William Carey for a World Missions' Conference to be held at the Cape of Good Hope in 1810. There were at that time no American overseas missionary societies functioning. The Board of Commissioners for Foreign Missions was founded in fact that very year. Ruth Rouse engages in a fascinating exercise of discovering who would and could have attended such a conference.

In the whole of *South America* it emerges that there were at that time no Protestant missionaries at all. One of the earliest, Captain Alan Gardiner (who died of hunger and exposure in September 1851 seeking to evangelize Patagonia and Tierra del Fuego), was still a midshipman in the British navy fighting against Napoleon.

In the whole of *Africa* there was only Dr Van Der Kemp of the London Missionary Society in the Cape (who would have acted as host to the conference) working with a small group of baptized Hottentots. In the rest of that great continent the only other Christian pockets that we know of were the liberated Christian slaves at Freetown, Sierra Leone, and the old Coptic church in Ethiopia, where Moravian missionaries had worked more recently. Liv-

[20] C. H. Spurgeon, *The Treasury of David* (expounding Psalm 86:9). (Evangelical Press, 1977).
[21] R. Rouse, 'William Carey's Pleasing Dream', *IRM*, April 1949.

ingstone wasn't born until 1813! And Moffatt did not reach Africa till 1817.

When we come to *Asia* the story is not so different. True, there were missionaries in India, and Carey and Marshman could have come from the Danish colony of Serampore; there were German missionaries of the Halle Mission sent out by the King of Denmark and the British East India Company chaplains, Claudius Buchanan and Henry Martyn. It was just too early for Adoniram Judson who commenced work in Burma in 1813 and for Robinson and Gottlob Brückner who started in Java in the same year. There were a few missionaries in the South Seas who had fled to Sydney from the Tahiti massacre (they couldn't go to Melbourne because it didn't yet exist!). In Australia, Samuel Marsden was trying to stir up interest in the Maori people on the islands of New Zealand, but the first service there, conducted by Marsden himself, did not take place until Christmas Day 1814. True, Robert Morrison had been in position in Canton since 1807, studying Chinese and translating the New Testament. But in those days of disease and uncertain voyages on sailing ships would Morrison ever have travelled all the way to the Cape of Good Hope specially for a conference? Carey himself had left England never to return in forty years of missionary service in India. Andrew Fuller rejected Carey's proposal as 'one of William's pleasing dreams'. The proposal was totally impracticable, not only because of the problem of getting there but because in the whole of the three great continents of South America, Africa and Asia there was only a tiny handful of Protestant missionaries and very few Christians indeed. Carey had himself laboured for five and a half years before the first convert in 1800.

The other day I was talking to Dr Algy Stanley-Smith, one of the co-founders of the Ruanda Mission, who was born in China in 1890, the son of one of the famous 'Cambridge Seven'. I suddenly realized that he was born only eighty years after Carey's proposed conference and was nearer to that date than to the present day. In other words, 1810 seems a very long time ago, until we make the simple calculation that it is only 168 years ago, or two life times of eight-four years.

From a Christian point of view the whole world has entirely changed. There are literally millions of Christians in the Third World.

The multi-racial church

We have already spoken of the ultimate goal of the perfection of the church. But we are now concerned with the stages by which this perfection is reached. When asked to rejoice in considering the possibility that Christ may return today it is even more in relation to the present state of the church that one's heart cries out, Not yet, Lord, the bride is not yet ready for you to come. She is more like a foolish virgin unprepared, a 'Cinderella' sitting dejectedly among the institutional ashes, suffering from serious loss of memory.[22]

Emerito P. Nacpil, the gifted Filipino theologian, has pictured the Western missionary movement as a midwife assisting at the birth of the Christian community in the Third World. But now the child is born there is no longer any need for the midwife.

> It has . . . performed with love and sacrifice and patience and hard work the role of guardian and trustee over the growing life of the child. But now the child is grown up. He is ready to enjoy his freedom as a son and to assume his rights and duties as an heir. The day of his independence and maturity has arrived. Therefore, all guardians and trustees must now withdraw. Their last and final and most fitting act as guardians and trustees is to allow the son to claim his rightful freedom and to assume his responsibility in managing his own affairs and inheritance. . . . For the missionary movement to do this one final act of self-abnegation would be the most fitting conclusion to a long and glorious career of self-

[22]See M. C. Griffiths, *Cinderella with Amnesia* (IVP, 1975).

oblation . . . This one final act of self-sacrifice on the part of modern missions is nothing less than the charter of freedom and life for the younger churches. In other words, the most *missionary* service a missionary under the present system can do today in Asia is to go home![23]

The assumption, you see, is that missions are a kind of scaffolding which, once the church is built, can be removed. But is the church built yet? I tremble to think what would have happened if everybody had accepted Nacpil's view. His reasons for this view relate to some tragic distortions of what missionary work really is. In his country missions are seen to represent Western money, technology, imperialism and racialism, and individual missionaries and ministers are called 'clerico-fascists'. It is a sad fact that there are some missions which still fail to observe indigenous principles, dominating the situation through their money and through the distribution of Christian aid. So many think of the missionary field as the target for missionary activity when it is in reality an unharvested field in which national Christian and international missionary labour side by side.

I think of a quiet missionary who has started four new congregations in Manila in the last four years. Should he rather have gone home? Or I think of an Anglican diocese where the bishop has twenty-six parishes under him. He has systematically encouraged all the evangelical, ordained Anglican missionaries of the Church Missionary Society and the Overseas Missionary Fellowship to depart from the diocese. At the time of writing only twenty of those parishes (some of them consisting of three or four small congregations) have incumbent ministers. At one point consecrated elements were being flown from the capital down to the southern extremity of the diocese. Does the existence of a national church, however small and weak and undermanned, however inadequate in

[23] E. P. Nacpil, 'Mission but not Missionaries', *IRM*, July 1971.

terms of reaching a whole country with the gospel, have some special significance by virtue of the erection of a few church buildings and of an ecclesiastical super-structure? Is the gospel really being effectively preached to the peoples of that nation and is that church in any real sense growing and making progress towards biblical goals?

Paul uses the illustration of a midwife (Gal. 4:19) when it is clear from the letter that he does not yet see his task as completed. Rather the ministry of 'apostles . . . prophets . . . evangelists . . . pastors and teachers, to equip the saints for the work of ministry in order to build up the body of Christ' is going to continue 'until we all attain to the unity of the faith, and of the knowledge of the Son of God' (Eph. 4:11–13).

We must try then to answer the question whether one mark of progress of missions is the planting of a national church and the withdrawal of foreign missions. This is a very common idea. A diocese in Africa recently decided that they wanted only young inexperienced missionaries and that once a missionary had completed one term of service he would be asked to return home for good. Apparently older and more experienced missionaries with a better knowledge of language and culture are seen as a threat to the independence of the indigenous church. This is tragic in every sense: tragic that national Christians should feel so threatened; tragic that foreign missionaries should be so unwise as to be seen as a threat; and tragic that real wisdom and experience and understanding are not better valued. Surely missionaries of the greatest experience and highest quality should be most valued.

By contrast, when the Indian Congress for Evangelism was held it was urged by some not only that missionaries should not be among the panel of speakers (and why indeed should they be?) but that they should not be allowed even to attend the meetings. A number of Indian Christians made strong protest by saying that the whole concept of a 'national church' was biblically dubious. The church of Jesus Christ is an international body made up

190

of men and women of many different nations. We must always think in terms of the church in Asia, in Africa, or in India, rather than talk about the Asian Church, the African Church or the Indian Church. The deliberate exclusion of brothers in Christ on the basis of race was a denial of the essence of the Christian church as described in Ephesians 2.

There is an eschatological problem with this view of an increasing degree of ethnic separation among Christians. Is it progress that all Christians return forthwith to their own countries so that the universal church may be broken down into discrete national units? Do we then expect the last trump suddenly to sound with, hey presto, 'a great multitude, which no-one could count, from every nation and all tribes and peoples and tongues, standing before the throne and before the Lamb' (Rev. 7:9)? Does this make sense? Would we not expect to see rather the international church of Jesus Christ becoming increasingly multi-racial? Certainly any observer walking in the streets of Berkeley, California, finds that about a third of the people on the street are black, another third Asian and only the remaining third appear to be Caucasian. This may be an extreme example but quite apart from the United States it is true also that many parts of Britain and Europe are becoming increasingly international. Not only West Indians and Pakistanis, but refugees and former displaced persons from the last major European war, Europeans in search of work, refugees from Cambodia and Vietnam, Spaniards and Turks: the multi-racial mix seems to be steadily increasing the world over.

Before Australia was discovered all swans were white. Twenty years ago when I first became a missionary it was generally true that all missionaries were also white. Today this is still *assumed* to be the case in a great deal of discussion about missions. But within our own missionary society we have missionaries from Korea, Japan, Taiwan, the Philippines, Hong Kong, Malaysia, Singapore, India, Fiji, a coloured South African and Maoris from New

Zealand (where two long life-times ago the gospel had not arrived at all). The gospel is correspondingly more credible. It is no longer a just charge that Christianity is an American or a white man's religion because the universality of the gospel is demonstrated by the character of the missionary body.

Ethnic or integrated churches

There has been much discussion recently of the relative merits of ethnic and integrated churches in relation to the expression by McGavran and others that 'people like to become Christians without crossing racial, linguistic or class barriers'. It is a fact of missionary life in Indonesia that denominations exist not along doctrinal divisions but on a basis of ethnic divisions, much as, in America, Reformed churches are predominantly Dutch, and Lutheran predominantly German or Scandivanian in origin; and just as the Episcopalian Church in Scotland is more English than Scottish, and so on. Certainly, while there are linguistic differences between congregations, the things that are said about the need for interpretation in Scripture normally require that a service is conducted where possible in one language only. It becomes very complicated if week after week a service has to employ two or more languages.

And yet in countries like ours the credibility and authenticity of the church of Christ need to be demonstrated in multi-racial communities. It is to the credit of both the Roman Catholic Church and of the Church of the Province in South Africa that they have never been segregated. Yet to demonstrate that the church is indeed a community of reconciliation is easier as an ideal than in practice at ground level. Many people feel easier in their own sub-cultural environment. It was tragic, for example, to learn that, when the Episcopal Church in Syracuse, New York, integrated its congregations most of the black members left and joined the Methodists. This is surely a problem we have to crack.

We must be careful not to force racial integration in situations that might hinder the growth of the church. In South Thailand, for example, the occasional Malay converts from Islam, with a different culture and a different language from the Thai, never seem to have been able to continue in the faith while belonging to a 99% Thai church. Once they were allowed to form their own separate Malay-speaking church, creating their own indigenous music from scratch, growth began to take place.

> An artificial attempt to break down barriers between men by eliminating or by-passing national and tribal differences may in the end be another type of ecclesiastical colonialism, an attempt to impose patterns of life on new peoples for which they are not prepared.[24]

Not everybody is willing to recognize this problem realistically, however, so that McGavran is criticized for the so-called 'homogeneous unit' principle when he urges that new churches cannot be brought together until 'the perfecting stage, when ethnic and cultural units have been discipled'.

In New Testament times there is evidence that some Jewish synagogues were divided by linguistic barriers. The solution must surely be never to exclude anyone from any church on the basis of race. But more than this, where there is a common language it is essential that we have model multi-racial congregations which are ahead of society as a whole and setting a pattern for inter-racial harmony and integration. We must prove the credibility of the church as a community of reconciliation by successfully holding together multi-racial congregations.

Patrick Sookdheo, working in Britain among immigrant inner city communities, has been planting new congregations which seem to preserve both the multi-racial identification of the church and the separate cultural identities

[24] Jordan Bishop, 'Numerical Growth – An Adequate Criterion of Mission?', *IRM*, July 1968, p.285.

of the separate segments of the congregations. The whole congregation is made up of people of several main ethnic identities – West Indians, Pakistanis, Indians and various white racial groups – and the united leadership is representative of these differing races, sharing the common vision of a multi-racial church. But the church also meets, as an extension of the housegroup principle, in smaller units of those who share a common background and culture. A new convert does not have to change his culture in order to become a Christian. Thus this model preserves cultural identity and multi-racial fellowship: and with the passage of time we may expect to see the walls of the separate segments breaking down from the centre outwards. The diagram below shows the concept:

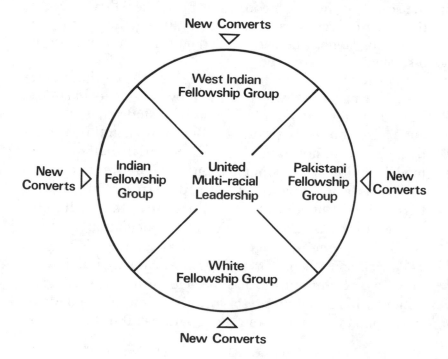

MULTI–RACIAL CONGREGATION

New Converts

West Indian
Fellowship Group

New
Converts

Indian
Fellowship
Group

United
Multi-racial
Leadership

Pakistani
Fellowship
Group

New
Converts

White
Fellowship Group

New Converts

In Southern Africa the multi-racial team of 'African Enterprise' seems to be effective in preaching the gospel from a multi-racial platform. Britain badly needs a similar kind of team available for work in areas where there are considerable immigrant communities.

Priesthood of all male believers?

Paul writes, 'There is neither Jew nor Greek, there is neither slave nor free man, there is neither male nor female; for you are all one in Christ Jesus' (Gal. 3:28). Not only do we expect racial distinctions to be broken down but we also expect sexual discrimination to be overcome. While Protestant churches have always given lip-service to the doctrine of the priesthood of all believers, and these days to the doctrine that all Christians are meant to be functioning members of the body, there have always been strong cultural factors which have relegated women to a secondary status both as 'priests' and 'members' of the body. This has been a cultural distortion of the Christian pattern.

It has traditionally been justified from some proof texts in Scripture (but then only 125 years ago earnest Christians were finding biblical support for slavery). As a church develops and approaches closer to the *parousia*, should we not expect an increase in its multi-racial character, the disappearance of its class barriers and a heightened realization that 'there is neither male nor female' as far as sexual discrimination within the church is concerned? It is often overlooked that there are in the New Testament several very positive passages about women's ministry in the New Testament church. In Philippians 4:3 Paul speaks of the women in Philippi who were members of the same team (*sunēthlēsan*) and fellow-workers (*sunergōn*) and in Romans 16 a remarkable number of women are mentioned as involved in some form of active ministry in the congregation. Phoebe is *diakonos* (verse 1) and *prostatis* (verse 2, a cognate word to those who lead in Rom. 12:8; 1 Thes. 5:12). Priscilla is *sunergos* (verse 3) while Mary (verse 6) Tryphena, Tryphosa and Persis (verse 12) all 'labour', a technical expression for Christian ministry used also of Paul and others. Chrysostom also understood Junia (verse 7) to be both a woman and an apostle. It is significant too that the word *anthrōpoi* rather than *androi* is used in 2 Timothy 2:2, leaving it open to the possibility of women teaching; 'thus hand it (everything I teach) on to reliable *people'* (Jerusalem Bible).

There needs therefore to be a much closer exegetical study of the more frequently quoted 'negative passages' about women's ministry: not because we want to evade the force of them, but because our doctrine of Scripture demands that we do so. We must find an acceptable interpretation of them that harmonizes with the positive passages. Thus 1 Timothy 2:12 may refer to the teaching and domineering over of husbands by their wives rather than to teaching by women in general; while 1 Corinthians 14:34–35 is not a total ban upon women's oral involvement in worship (in the context, see verses 26, 31), but commands that questions which could equally be asked at home should not be allowed to disturb the meeting. All these passages are capable of a more positive exegesis. But until male Christians as a whole are convinced of this the woman's role may remain that of producing cups of tea and meals for the congregation!

It is interesting that from within the Roman Catholic context Karl Rahner can write,

> The question might be raised whether today or at least tomorrow, in the light of the secular social situation, a woman could be considered just as much as a man for leadership of a basic community and therefore could be ordained to the priestly office. Having in mind the society of today and even more of tomorrow, I see no reason in principle to give a negative answer to this question.[25]

In a climate where the whole question of the ministry

[25] K. Rahner, *The Shape of the Church to Come* (SPCK, 1974) p.114.

of women is under discussion, as well as woman's traditional role in society, as captive housewife/homemaker, the church entrusted with the liberating gospel (which allowed women to be disciples, to sit at the feet of Jesus and to be taught, in radical discontinuity with contemporary Judaism) needs to decide today what priesthood in biblical terms and membership of the body mean for women. Certainly we know that according to the words of Jesus, 'those who are considered worthy to attain to that age and the resurrection from the dead, neither marry, nor are given in marriage; for neither can they die any more, for they are like angels, and are sons of God, being sons of the resurrection' (Lk. 20:35–36) Thus in heaven the child-bearing, home-making roles would seem to be done away with. In parallel with the ending of discrimination based on social and racial grounds, should we not experience in the church the disappearance of discrimination based upon sexual distinctions and expect instead an increasing emancipation of women from their traditional cultural bondage as the anticipated fruit of redemption in Christ? It can be argued that the sexes were created originally with parity (Gn. 1:27) and that subjection is only relevant to the marriage relationship (Gn. 2:22–24). It seems unlikely that Christians are to regard all women as bone of their bone and flesh of their flesh! It is this fatal confusion which arises from trying to make the subjection of a wife to her husband mean the subjection of all women to all men which befuddles much recent discussion.[26] Some see discussion of the role of women as a controversial sidetrack. But if the liberating of Christian women from cultural bondage is an essential part of the perfecting of the church, we cannot ignore it.

[26] See Peter Moore (ed.), *Man, Woman and Priesthood* (SPCK, 1978) for interesting illustrations of cultural presuppositions.

An increasing breakdown of clericalism

The introduction of hierarchical notions into Christianity is another cultural distortion which Jesus himself had already decisively rejected (Mt. 23:8–10). Clericalism frequently derives from underlying animistic or folk beliefs which preceded the introduction of the Christian gospel. Thus the guru in India, the shaman in Korea and the sensei in Japan are all to some extent perpetuated in the clerical notions of their respective national churches. In the West the Protestant minister certainly owes something to the Roman Catholic priest who preceded him before the Reformation, and the Catholic priest a good deal to the druid who preceded Augustine and Columba.

It is interesting that in the Roman Catholic context Karl Rahner sees the church of the future as a 'declericalised church'. He explains this by saying that it is to be

> a church in which the office-holders too, in joyous humility, allow for the fact that the Spirit breathes where he will and that he has not arranged an exclusive and permanent tenancy with them. They recognize that the charismatic element, which can never be completely regulated, is just as necessary as office to the church; that office is never simply identical with the Spirit and can never replace him; that office too is really effectively credible in the sight of men only when the presence of the Spirit is evident and not merely when formal mission and authority are invoked however legitimate these may be.[27]

Rahner also rather amusingly reminds us that 'the pastor should remain a pastor, but this certainly does not mean that he should treat his flock as if they really were sheep'.[28]

This breakdown of clericalism is increasingly evident even in what was once regarded as such a bastion of sacerdotalism as the Church of the Province in South Africa. The increasing practice of having so-called 'lay-

[27] Rahner, *op. cit.*, p.27.
[28] *Ibid.*, p.121.

men' distributing the elements in both kinds shows that the tendency to regard ordination as conveying almost magical powers to a 'priest' is increasingly fading away. A more positive and biblical teaching that professional ministers are exercising one role within the complete laity of God rather than occupying a hierarchical upper story should all help to accelerate the departure of the one-man-band view of the ministry. Old habits and attitudes die hard, however: it is one thing to make theological assertions and another thing for clergy deliberately to refuse such distinctions of dress and deference which perpetuate unscriptural divisions. Thus the National Evangelical Anglican Congress held in Nottingham in April 1977 said,

> Clerical professionalism has gravely inhibited the proper development of the diversity of ministries. We deplore the prevalent pattern of 'one man ministries,' which are good neither for the man nor for the parish, and we call on parishes to work towards shared leadership.[29]

But there is a great difference between producing high-sounding declarations of this kind and actually implementing them in the church. It is not enough to deplore clericalism. We would anticipate its disappearance to be one of the marks of the church's preparation for the *parousia*.

Increasing unity of the visible church

Paul does not seem to have had to wrestle with the problems of denominationalism though he is constantly needing to give encouragements to unity (Eph. 4:3; Phil. 1:27; 2:2, *etc.*). Even when facing churches with manifestly heterodox views (1 Cor. 15:12 and Gal. 1:6) he nowhere suggests the setting up of a new orthodox 'denomination', but rather expects that the church will, under the guidance of the Spirit, restore those who are in error and

---

[29] *The Nottingham Statement* (Falcon, 1977), J2, p.33.

return from its deviation to the true way. He did, of course, have to deal with the problem of factions arising very early in the history of the Corinthian church (1 Cor. 1:12 ff.).

The essential problem relates to the matters discussed in our second chapter. *There has to be a dealing with all the cultural distortions and historical deviations that have arisen in the course of church history* as a result of taking the gospel to all nations. This is the task of 'indigenous theology' to de-indigenize the cultural distortions and to bring us to the unity of the faith. This is perfecting the church.

The perfecting of the church must include the unity of the faith – we cannot ignore this. Paul anticipates the ultimate goal as arrival 'at the unity of the faith' (Eph. 4:13) as well as requiring diligence to preserve the unity of the Spirit (Eph. 4:3).

The tragic reductionism of the ecumenical movement, which has totally alienated large sections of evangelical opinion, seems to have de-accelerated as a result of the inclusion of the Eastern Orthodox churches. Currently the temper and climate of the ecumenical movement still seem far away from the days of the great doctrinal confessions like the Augsburg and Westminster Confessions. Perhaps we are being unduly optimistic to anticipate that, as secularism and theological radicalism effectively reduce the numbers within the church, the believing remnant will increasingly be of one mind on the essential core of biblical doctrine. Church history bears adequate testimony to the fact that theological radicalism has few children and no grandchildren. Heterodox mutations are almost always lethal for when there is little good news left to proclaim there remains little motivation for proclaiming the attentuated residue.

While the attempt to produce church union on a major scale seems to get bogged down in interminable negotiation over details, we may anticipate seeing on a local level the increasing breakdown of barriers between traditional denominational churches and congregations coming together in town-wide and city-wide groupings. This is what Rahner calls the 'church from the roots' when he says that

> the church of the future will be one built from below by basic communities as a result of free initiative and association. We should make every effort not to hold up, but to promote this development and direct it on to the right lines . . . the church will exist only by being constantly renewed by a free decision of faith and the formation of congregations on the part of individuals in the midst of a secular society bearing no imprint of Christianity.[30]

The way ahead

We need to pray not only for renewal but also for revival in the church. The Lausanne Covenant declares:

> World-wide evangelization will become a realistic possibility only when the Spirit renews the church in truth and wisdom, faith, holiness, love, and power. We, therefore, call upon all Christians to pray for such a visitation of the sovereign Spirit of God that all his fruit may appear in all his people and that all his gifts may enrich the body of Christ. Only then will the whole church become a fit instrument in his hands, that the whole earth may hear his voice.[31]

It certainly seems that such 'times of refreshing' (*kairoi anapsuxeōs*, Acts 3:20) must inevitably precede the 'times of restoration of all things' (*chronōn apokatastaseōs*, Acts 3:21). It is precisely the possibility of revival that delivers us from pessimism and helps us to realize that God in his sovereignty is able to bless and to quicken his church in times of institutional formalism and spiritual coldness and backsliding. When one is privileged to visit churches which have seen a spiritual quickening in revival, as in some of the Sarawak longhouses, one is

---

[30] Rahner, *op. cit.*, p.108.
[31] Clause 14 'The Power of the Holy Spirit', *LTEHHV*, p.8.

thrilled and delighted to find a combination of simple lifestyle, communal living and spiritual refreshing.

Such blessing does not come without battle and conflict. Revival often seems to be the precursor of persecution, strengthening the church to face opposition. It is certainly clear that the New Testament sees Satan and the spiritual forces of wickedness plucking up the seed, planting tares, laying snares for Christians and generally carrying out a war on the saints. It does need to be recognized that there are hostile forces working against the church not only from without but also from within. Paul Tillich expresses this clearly:

> In history there is a continuous mixture of good and evil in every group, in every agency that carries the historical process, in every period, in every historical actualization . . . The historical representative of the kingdom of God, in so far as it *fights in* history, is the Christian church. The Christian church, the embodiment of the New Being in a community, represents the kingdom of God. The church itself is not the kingdom of God but it is its agent, its anticipation, its fragmentary realization. It is *fighting* in history, and since it represents the kingdom of God it can be distorted but it can never be conquered.[32]

At the same time it is to be realized that progress need not necessarily be slow and gradual, as congregation after congregation oscillates between blessing and renewal on the one hand and regress, coldness and backsliding on the other. Paul says of the Thessalonians that they 'became an example to all the believers in Macedonia and in Achaia' (1 Thes. 1:7). If we can establish congregations which become patterns for others who will want to follow their example, we will see churches over whole provinces being renewed and transformed in a generation. Is this

[32] Paul Tillich, 'Mission and World History' in G. H. Anderson (ed.) *The Theology of the Christian Mission*, p.282.

the task that God plans to give to you as you prepare for Christian ministry?

Tetullian tells us that Christians were called a *genus tertius* and that they were called 'the new people . . . *the people of the future*'.[33] As we have seen above, this faith in the future, this eschatological hope, depends upon firm doctrinal conviction. 'Wishy-washy' Christians will achieve little or nothing. It demands a faith like William Carey's to 'expect great things from God and to attempt great things for God'. Let me close with a quotation from Hans Küng, a prayer from the *Didache* (quoted by him) and a verse from Scripture.

> Has the Church a future, a future in this modern world? This was the question we asked ourselves at the beginning. The fundamental answer has already been given: *if* the Church believes, preaches and lives, convincingly and actively, the message of Jesus Christ, then it has a future in the modern world and in humanity. For then it will be granted not *a* future, above and beyond any modern age, but *the* future, the only perfect future: the kingdom of God. No one can promise or grant more.[34]

> Remember O Lord, your Church,
> save it from every evil
> and perfect it in your love.
> Gather it together from the four winds
> and lead it sanctified
> into your Kingdom you have prepared for it.[35]

> For I know the plans that I have for you, declares the Lord, plans for welfare and not for calamity to give you a future and a hope.[36]

Let us commit ourselves afresh to this task as fellow workers with God.

[33] Adolf Harnack, *The Mission and Expansion of Christianity in the First Three Centuries* (2 vols., 1908), Vol. 1, p.204 ff.

[34] Hans Küng, *The Church* (Search Press, 1968), p.103.

[35] *Didache*, 10:5.

[36] Je. 29:11.

Material for study

Ruth Rouse, 'William Carey's Pleasing Dream', *IRM*, April 1949.

Oscar Cullmann, 'Eschatology and Missions in the New Testament', and

Paul Tillich, 'Mission and World History' in G. H. Anderson (ed.), *The Theology of the Christian Mission* (SCM Press, 1961).

Iain Murray, *The Puritan Hope* (Banner of Truth, 1971).

Michael Griffiths, *Cinderella with Amnesia* (IVP, 1975).

Questions for discussion

1. What intermediate steps do you anticipate as the church advances towards the *parousia?*

2. What do you regard as the most hopeful advances in the present century towards the goal of a perfected church?

3. How do you relate the expectation of delay in the return of the king (Lk. 19:11) with the expectation of the Lord's imminent return? How do these two apparently conflicting ideas in fact leave room for the good steward to attempt great things for God, his royal master? Discuss the danger of quietism or absence of long-term planning in some dispensational positions.

4. Do moratoria and 'missionary go home' attitudes tie in with biblical views of mission? What is the finishing-point for the missionary who wants to run the race as Paul did?

5. Discuss ways in which doctrinal swings within the church as a whole have affected missionary enthusiasm (*e.g.* theological liberalism, dispensational premillennialism, social gospel *etc.*).

6. Pray about your own future ministry in planting and perfecting churches.

Appendix

The biblical language of pastoralia

H. B. Swete in his commentary on the Apocalypse of St John drops an interesting hint when he says that *'stērizein, like bebaioun* and *themelioun,* is a technical word in primitive pastoralia'.[1] In the New Testament different Greek verbs describe the activities of the first missionaries. When we study these words we learn how the apostles regarded their work of establishing congregations and what concepts concerned them most. What verbs are used to describe their activity? There is not space here for a full treatment, but they fall into three main groups.

1. Church planting words (or foundation words)

   i.   *themelioō* is a verb related to the noun *themelios,* used of laying a foundation (1 Cor. 3:10–11), and of the foundation of the city which God builds (Heb. 11:10). The verb is used for the wise man who built his house on the rock (Mt. 7:25) and in a church planting sense of grounding and establishing (Eph. 3:17; Col. 1:23; 1 Pet. 5:10).

   ii.   *rhizoō,* to cause to take root, fix firmly and (pass.) to be firmly rooted, is used in Ephesians 3:17

[1] H. B. Swete, *The Apocalypse of St John* (Macmillan, third edition, 1911).

('rooted and grounded') and in Colossians 2:7 where there seems to be a deliberate sequence, 'having been firmly rooted, now being built up and being made firm in your faith'. Lest we see being grounded in Christ as mechanical juxtaposition, we are reminded we need an organic relationship, in which we draw our life from him. We need to plant.

2. Church building words (or continuing words)

i. *oikodomeō* is used of building both literally and figuratively. While to us building is a short-term project, Deissmann[2] reminds us that ancient temples, like medieval cathedrals, might be in the course of construction for hundreds of years. Jesus 'builds' his church (Mt. 16:18); the churches were being 'built up' (Acts 9:31) from living stones (1 Pet. 2:5). This word, and its cognates, is used several times in 1 Corinthians 14 of the building up (edification) of the congregation.

ii. *epoikodomeō* means to build upon (a foundation) and is used in 1 Corinthians 3:10; Colossians 2:7 and Ephesians 2:20.

iii. *sunoikodomeō* is used of the Holy Spirit's action in building us together (Eph. 2:22) into the fabric of the living church.

iv. *sunarmologeō* (Eph. 2:21; 4:16) means to fit or join together.

v. *sumbibazō* means to knit together (Eph. 4:16; Col. 2:2), so that again the building metaphor is reinforced with a biological one – Christians in the church are not just to be in adjacent pews, but organically related.

These ideas of 'building up' are predominantly congregational and corporate. 'Follow-

---

[2] Adolf Deissmann, *Light from the Ancient East* (Harper, 1922).

up', in our jargon, involves much more individual self-development whereas in biblical terminology it is seen as congregation building.

vi.   *auxanō*, to grow, is most frequently what God causes to happen (1 Cor. 3:6; Eph. 2:21; 4:15; Col. 1:6, 10; 1 Pet. 2:2 and 2 Pet. 3:18).

3. Church perfecting words (or finishing words)

i.   *stērizō*, to establish, is derived from the word *sterinx* meaning a support. It means to fix something so that it will stand upright and immovable. It is used of Jesus in 'setting' his face to go to Jerusalem, of strengthening disciples (Acts 18:23) and churches (1 Thes. 3:2, 13). This is what an established church is in biblical terms – one that will stand. The intensive form *epistērizō* also occurs in Acts 14:22; 15:32, 41.

ii.   *katartizō* means to render *artios* (*i.e.* efficient or capable). So it means to equip or make capable of fulfilling the function for which it was made (Mt. 4:21; 1 Cor. 1:10; Gal. 6:1; Eph. 4:12; 1 Thes. 3:10; Heb. 13:2; 1 Pet. 5:10). It is frequently used of the church being perfected.

iii. *bebaioō* is to make firm or establish (1 Cor. 1:8; 2 Cor. 1:21; Col. 2:7). It will be seen that many of this group of words focus on the expectation of the Lord's return: through this fixing, completing and establishing the congregation is prepared for the Lord's return.

These verbs (and their cognate nouns) describe first-century apostolic activity in building the church. This language does not adequately describe much of what passes in ecumenical circles for missionary activity today.